PREFACES TO SHAKESPEARE

Books *by* Harley Granville-Barker

Plays.

The Marrying of Ann Leete.
The Voysey Inheritance.   (Revised 1913.)
Waste.   (Rewritten 1926.)
The Madras House.   (Revised 1925.)
Rococo: Vote by Ballot: Farewell to the Theatre.
   (Three one-act plays.)   1917.
The Secret Life.   1923.
His Majesty.   1928.

With LAURENCE HOUSMAN

Prunella: or, Love in a Dutch Garden.   (Revised
   1930.)

With DION CLAYTON CALTHROP.

The Harlequinade.   1918.

English Versions of Foreign Plays.

Anatol: *by* Arthur Schnitzler.   1911.
Doctor Knock: *by* Jules Romains.   1925.
Six Gentlemen in a Row: *by* Jules Romains.   1927.

With HELEN GRANVILLE-BARKER.

The Kingdom of God: *by* Gregorio Martinez Sierra.
   1927.
The Romantic Young Lady: *by* the same.   1929.
Take Two from One: *by* the same.   1931.
The Women have their Way: A Hundred Years Old:
   Fortunato: The Lady from Alfaqueque: *by*
   Serafín and Joaquín Alvarez Quintero.   1927.
Love Passes By: Don Abel wrote a Tragedy: Peace
   and Quiet: Doña Clarines: *by* the same.   1932.

Criticism.

The Exemplary Theatre.   1922.
From Henry V. to Hamlet.
Prefaces to Shakespeare: First Series.   1927.
Prefaces to Shakespeare: Second Series.   1930.
Prefaces to Shakespeare: Third Series.   1937.
The Use of the Drama.   1946.
On Dramatic Method.   1931.

Sidgwick & Jackson, Ltd.

PREFACES TO SHAKESPEARE

BY
HARLEY
GRANVILLE-BARKER

First Series

LONDON: SIDGWICK & JACKSON, LTD.
44 MUSEUM STREET   1946

First published	1927
Second impression	1933
Third impression	1940
Fourth impression	1945
Fifth impression	1946

Richard Clay and Company, Ltd., Printers, Bungay, Suffolk.

THESE three Prefaces—and others to follow—were
first written for *The Players' Shakespeare*; and I
have to thank the publishers of those fine volumes
(Messrs. Ernest Benn Limited) for facilitating the
reappearance of my share in them. I have now
been able to revise the work in the light of the
criticism it has received, and of my own (I
hope) better judgment. The prefaces to *Love's
Labour's Lost* and *Julius Cæsar* have, indeed, been
largely re-written, and the Introduction is practically new.

I have made much use of the *Arden Shakespeare*,
and my lineal references are to that text; much
use also—as who does not?—of the Furness
Variorum. With *Love's Labour's Lost* I had the advantage of Dr. Dover Wilson's work for the new
Cambridge Shakespeare, and I have profited by Mr.
W. J. Lawrence's studies of the Elizabethan
playhouse. No one, approaching Shakespearean
criticism from this angle, should omit his tribute
to Richard G. Moulton's virile pioneering. To
A. C. Bradley, Dr. Pollard and Sir Edmund
Chambers (whose work is a rock on which to build
and in which to quarry), I owe the debt all
students of Shakespeare owe nowadays; and to
Sir Mark Hunter great gratitude for acute and
kindly criticism—which led me, in particular, to
reconsider *Julius Cæsar* carefully.

H. G.-B.

August 1927

CONTENTS

CONTENTS

INTRODUCTION

W<small>E</small> have still much to learn about Shakespeare the playwright. Strange that it should be so, after three centuries of commentary and performance, but explicable. For the Procrustean methods of a changed theatre deformed the plays, and put the art of them to confusion; and scholars, with this much excuse, have been apt to divorce their Shakespeare from the theatre altogether, to think him a poet whose use of the stage was quite incidental, whose glory had small relation to it, for whose lapses it was to blame.

THE STUDY AND THE STAGE

This much is to be said for Garrick and his predecessors and successors in the practice of reshaping Shakespeare's work to the theatre of their time. The essence of it was living drama to them, and they meant to keep it alive for their public. They wanted to avoid whatever would provoke question and so check that spontaneity of response upon which acted drama depends. Garrick saw the plays, with their lack of ‘ art,’ through the spectacles of contemporary culture; and the bare Elizabethan stage, if it met his mind's eye at all, doubtless as a barbarous make-shift. Shakespeare was for him a problem ; he tackled it, from our point of view, misguidedly and with an overplus of enthusiasm. His was a positive world ; too near in time, moreover, as well as too opposed in taste to Shakespeare's to treat it perspectively. The romantic movement might have brought a more concordant outlook. But by then the scholars were off their own way; while the theatre began to think of its Shakespeare from the point of view of the picturesque, and, later, in terms of upholstery. Nineteenth-century drama developed along the lines of realistic illusion, and the staging of Shakespeare was further subdued to this, with inevitably disastrous effect on the speaking of his verse; there was less perversion of text perhaps, but actually more wrenching of the construction of the plays for the convenience of the stage carpenter. The public appetite for this sort of thing having been gorged, producers then turned to newer—and older—contrivances, leaving 'realism' (so called) to the modern comedy that had fathered it. Amid much vaporous theorising—but let us humbly own how hard it is not to write nonsense about art, which seems ever pleading to be enjoyed and not written about at all—the surprising discovery had been made that varieties of stagecraft and stage were not historical accidents but artistic actualities, that Greek drama belonged in a Greek theatre, that Elizabethan plays, therefore, would, presumably, go best upon an Elizabethan stage, that there was nothing sacrosanct about scenery, footlights, drop-curtain or any of their belongings. This brings us to the present situation.

There are few enough Greek theatres in which Greek tragedy can be played; few enough people want to see it, and they will applaud it encouragingly however it is done. Some acknowledgment is due to the altruism of the doers! Shakespeare is another matter. The English theatre, doubtful of its destiny, of necessity venal, opening its doors to all comers, seems yet, as by some instinct, to seek renewal of strength in him. An actor, till success has made him cynical, or if his talent be not merely trivial, may take some pride in the hall-mark of Shakespearean achievement. So may a manager if he thinks he can afford it. The public (or their spokesmen) seem to consider Shakespeare and his genius a sort of national property, which, truly, they do nothing to conserve, but in which they have moral rights not lightly to be flouted. The production of the plays is thus still apt to be marked by a timid respect for " the usual thing " ; their acting is crippled by pseudo-traditions, which are inert because they are not Shakespearean at all. They are the accumulation of two centuries of progressive misconception and distortion of his playwright's art. On the other hand, England has been spared production of Shakespeare according to this or that even more irrelevant theory of presentationalism, symbolism, constructivism or what not. There is the breach in the wall of ' realism,' but we have not yet made up our minds to pass through, taking our Shakespeare with us.

Incidentally, we owe the beginning of the breach to Mr. William Poel, who, with fanatical courage, when ' realism ' was at the tottering height of its triumph in the later revivals of Sir Henry Irving, and the yet more richly upholstered revelations of Sir Herbert Tree, thrust the Elizabethan stage in all its apparent eccentricity upon our unwilling notice.[1] Mr. Poel shook complacency. He could

[1] But it should not be forgotten that Sir Herbert Tree, happy in the orthodoxy of public favour, welcomed the heretic Mr. Poel more than once to a share in his Shakespeare Festivals.

not expect to do much more; for he was a logical reformer. He showed us the Elizabethan stage, with Antony and Cleopatra, Troilus and Cressida, in their ruffs and farthingales as for Shakespeare's audiences they lived. Q.E.D. There, however, as far as the popular theatre was concerned, the matter seemed to rest for twenty years or so. But it was just such a demonstration that was needed; anything less drastic and provocative might have been passed over with mild approval.

To get the balance true, let us admit that while Shakespeare was an Elizabethan playwright he was—and now is to us—predominantly something much more. Therefore we had better not too unquestioningly thrust him back within the confines his genius has escaped, nor presume him to have felt the pettier circumstances of his theatre sacrosanct. Nor can we turn Elizabethans as we watch the plays; and every mental effort to do so will subtract from our enjoyment of them. This is the case against the circumstantial reproduction of Shakespeare's staging. But Mr. Poel's achievement remains; he cleared for us from Shakespeare's stagecraft the scenic rubbish by which it had been so long encumbered and disguised. And we could now, if we would, make a promising fresh start. For the scholars, on their side, have lately —the scholarly among them—cut clear of the transcendental fog (scenic illusion of another sort) in which their nineteenth-century peers loved to lose themselves, and they too are beginning again at the beginning. A text acquires virtue now by its claim to be a prompt book, and the most comprehensive work of our time upon the Elizabethan stage is an elaborate sorting out of plays, companies and theatres. On Dr. Pollard's treatment of the texts and on the foundations of fact laid by Sir Edmund Chambers a new scholarship is rising, aiming first to see Shakespeare in the theatre for which he wrote. It is a scholarship, therefore, by which the theatre of to-day can profit, to which, by its acting of Shakespeare, it could contribute, one would hope. Nor should the scholars disdain the help; for criticism cannot live upon criticism, it needs refreshment from the living art. Besides, what is all the criticism and scholarship finally for if not to keep Shakespeare alive? And he must always be most alive—even if roughly and rudely alive—in the theatre. Let the scholars force a way in there, if need be. Its fervid atmosphere will do them good; the benefit will be mutual.

These prefaces are an attempt to profit by this new scholarship and to contribute to it some research into Shakespeare's stagecraft, by examining the plays, one after another, in the light of the interpretation he designed for them, so far as this can be deduced or imagined; to discover, if possible, the production he would have desired for them, all merely incidental circumstances apart. They might profit more written a generation hence, for the ground they build upon is still far from clear. And this Introduction is by no means a conspectus of the subject; that can only come as a sequel. There has been, in this branch of Shakespearean study, too much generalisation and far too little analysis of material.[1]

---

[1] I do not deal in general therefore with certain vexed questions, such as Act-division, which still need to be looked at, I think, in the light of the particular play.

INTRODUCTION

SHAKESPEARE'S STAGECRAFT

Shakespeare's own career was not a long one. The whole history of the theatre he wrote for does not cover a century. Between Marlowe and Massinger, from the first blaze to the glowing of the embers, it is but fifty years. Yet even while Shakespeare was at work, the stage to which he fitted his plays underwent constant and perhaps radical change. From Burbage's first theatre to the Globe, then to Blackfriars, not to mention excursions to Court and into the great halls— change of audiences and their behaviour, of their taste, development of the art of acting, change of the stage itself and its resources were all involved in the progress, and are all, we may be sure, reflected to some degree in the plays themselves. We guess at the conditions of each sort of stage and theatre, but there is often the teasing question to which of them had a play, as we have it now, been adapted. And of the ' private ' theatre, most in vogue for the ten years preceding the printing of the First Folio, so far we know least. The dating of texts and their ascription to the usages of a particular theatre may often be a searchlight upon their stagecraft. Here is much work for the new scholarship.

Conversely, the watchful working out of the plays in action upon this stage or that would be of use to the scholars, who otherwise must reconstruct their theatres and gloss their texts as in a vacuum. The play was once fitted to the stage; it is by no means impossible to rebuild that stage now, with its doors, balconies, curtains and machines, by measuring the needs of the play. It is idle, for instance, to imagine scenes upon inner or upper stage without evidence that they will be audible or

visible there ; and editing is still vitiated by lack
of this simple knowledge. Here, if nowhere else,
this present research must fall short, for its method
should rightly be experimental ; more than one
mind should be at work on it, moreover.

The text of a play is a score waiting performance, and the performance and its preparation are,
almost from the beginning, a work of collabora-
tion. A producer may direct the preparation,
certainly. But if he only knows how to give
orders, he has mistaken his vocation ; he had better
be a drill-sergeant. He might talk to his company
when they all met together for the first time to
study *Love's Labour's Lost*, *Julius Cæsar*, or *King Lear*,
on some such lines as these prefaces pursue, giving
a considered opinion of the play, drawing a picture
of it in action, providing, in fact, a hypothesis
which mutual study would prove—and might
partly disprove. No sort of study of a play can
better the preparation of its performance if this is
rightly done. The art of the playwright lies in
giving life to characters in action, and the secret
of it in giving each character a due chance in the
battle, the action of a play being literally the
fighting of a battle of character. So the greater
the playwright, the wider and deeper his sym-
pathies, the more genuine this opposition will be
and the less easily will a single mind grasp it, as
it must be grasped, in the fullness of its emotion.
The dialogue of a play runs—and often intricately
—upon lines of reason, but it is charged besides with
an emotion which speech releases, yet only releases
fully when the speaker is—as an actor is—identified
with the character. There is further the incidental action, implicit in the dialogue, which

springs to life only when a scene is in being. A play, in fact, as we find it written, is a magic spell; and even the magician cannot always foresee the full effect of it.

Not every play, it must be owned, will respond to such intensive study. Many, ambitiously conceived, would collapse under the strain. Many are mere occasions for display of their actors' wit or eloquence, good looks or nice behaviour, and meant to be no more; and if they are skilfully contrived the parts fit together and the whole machine should go like clockwork. Nor, in fact, are even the greatest plays often so studied. There is hardly a theatre in the world where masterpiece and trumpery alike are not rushed through rehearsals to an arbitrarily effective performance, little more learnt of them than the words, gaps in the understanding of them filled up with ' business '—effect without cause, the demand for this being the curse of the theatre as of other arts, as of other things than art. Not to such treatment will the greater plays of Shakespeare yield their secrets. But working upon a stage which reproduced the essential conditions of his, working as students, not as showmen merely, a company of actors might well find many of the riddles of the library answering themselves unasked. And these prefaces could best be a record of such work, if such work were to be done.

We cannot, on the other hand, begin our research by postulating the principles of the Elizabethan stage. One is tempted to say it had none, was too much a child of nature to bother about such things. Principles were doubtless imposed upon it when it reached respectability, and heads would be bowed to the yoke. Shakespeare's among them? He had served a most practical apprenticeship to his trade. If he did not hold horses at the door, he sat behind the curtain, we may be sure, and held the prompt book on occasion. He acted, he cobbled other men's plays, he could write his own to order. Such an one may stay a journeyman if he is not a genius, but he will not become a doctrinaire. Shakespeare's work shows such principles as the growth of a tree shows. It is not haphazard merely because it is not formal; it is shaped by inner strength. The theatre, as he found it, allowed him and encouraged him to great freedom of development. Because the material resources of a stage are simple, it does not follow that the technique of its playwriting will stay so. Crude work may show up more crudely, when there are none of the fal-lals of illusion to disguise it that the modern theatre provides. But, if he has it in him, a dramatist can, so unfettered, develop the essentials of his art more boldly and more subtly too. The Elizabethan drama made an amazingly quick advance from crudity to an excellence which was often technically most elaborate. The advance and the not less amazing gulf which divides its best from its worst may be ascribed to the simplicity of the machinery it employed. That its decadence was precipitated by the influence of the Mask and the shifting of its centre of interest from the barer public stage to the candle-lit private theatre, where the machinery of the Mask became effective, it would be rash to assert; but the occurrences are suspiciously related. Man and machine (here at any rate is a postulate, if a platitude!) are false allies in the theatre, secretly at odds; and when man gets the worst of it, drama is im-

poverished; and the struggle, we may add, is
perennial. No great drama depends upon
pageantry. All great drama tends to concentrate
upon character; and, even so, not upon picturing
men as they show themselves to the world like figures
on a stage—though that is how it must ostensibly
show them—but on the hidden man. And the progress of Shakespeare's art from *Love's Labour's Lost*
to *Hamlet*, and thereafter with a difference, lies in
the simplifying of this paradox and the solving
of the problem it presents; and the process
involves the developing of a very subtle sort of
stagecraft indeed.

For one result we have what we may call a very
self-contained drama. Its chief values, as we know,
have not changed with the fashions of the theatre.
It relies much on the music of the spoken word,
and a company of schoolchildren with pleasant
voices, and an ear for rhythm may shout through
a play to some effect. It is as much to be enjoyed
in the reading, if we sound it in imagination, as
true drama can be. As with its simplicities then,
so it should be, we presume, with its complexities.
The subtly emotional use of verse and the interplay of motive and character, these surely can be
appreciated apart from the bare boards of their
original setting! It does not follow. It neither
follows that the advantages of the Elizabethan
stage were wholly negative nor that, with our
present knowledge, we can imagine the full effect
of a play in action upon it. The imagining of a
play in action is, under no circumstances, an easy
thing.[1] What would one not give to go backward

---

[1] I remember a most intelligent reader of a modern play
missing the whole point of a scene through which the chief

through the centuries to see the first performance
of *Hamlet*, played as Shakespeare had it played.[1]
In default, if we could but make ourselves read it
as if it were a manuscript fresh from its author's
hands! There is much to be said for turning one's
back on the editors, even, when possible, upon the
First Folio with its demarcation of acts and scenes,
in favour of the Quartos—Dr. Pollard's 'good'
Quartos—in their yet greater simplicity.

THE CONVENTION OF PLACE

It is, for instance, hard to discount the impression
made merely by reading " Scene i—Elsinore. A
platform before the Castle "; and most of us have,
to boot, early memories of painted battlements
and tenth-century castles, of ageing Hamlets and
their portly mothers for that matter, very difficult
to dismiss. No great harm, one protests; it was
a help, perhaps, to the unimaginative. But it is
a first step to the certain misunderstanding of
Shakespeare's stagecraft. The 'if, how, and
when' of the presenting of localities on the Elizabethan stage is, of course, a complex question.
Shakespeare himself seems to have followed, consciously, no principles in the matter, nor was his

---

character was to sit conspicuously and eloquently silent.
He counted only with the written dialogue. I remember,
when I thought I knew *King Lear* well enough, being amazed
at the effect, all dialogue apart, of the mere meeting, when
I saw it, of blind Gloucester and mad Lear.

[1] Though, in a sense, there was no first performance of
Hamlet. And doubtless many of the audience for Shakespeare's new version of the old play only thought he had spoilt
a good story of murder and revenge by adding too much
talk to it.

practice very logical, nor at all consistent. It may vary with the play he is writing and the particular stage he is writing for; it will best be studied in relation to each play. We can, however, free ourselves from one general misconception which belongs to our own over-logical standpoint. When we learn with a shock of surprise—having begun in the schoolroom upon the Shakespeare of the editors, it comes as belated news to us— that neither battlements, throne rooms, nor picturesque churchyards were to be seen at the Globe, and that " Elsinore. A platform before the Castle " is not Shakespeare at all, we yet imagine ourselves among the audience there busily conjuring these things up before the eye of faith. The Elizabethan audience was at no such pains. Nor was this their alternative to seeing the actors undisguisedly concerned with the doors, curtains and balconies which, by the play's requirements, should have been anything but what they were. As we, when a play has no hold on us, may fall to thinking about the scenery, so to a Globe audience, unmoved, the stage might be an obvious bare stage. But are we conscious of the scenery behind the actor when the play really moves us? If we are, there is something very wrong with the scenery, which should know its place as a background. The audience was not conscious of curtain and balcony when Burbage played Hamlet to them. They were conscious of Hamlet. That conventional background faded as does our painted illusion, but they certainly did not deliberately conjure up in its place mental pictures of Elsinore. The genus audience is passive, if expectant, imaginatively lazy till roused; never, one may be sure, at pains to make any effort that is generally unnecessary to enjoyment.

With Shakespeare the locality of a scene has dramatic importance, or it has none; and this is as true of his early plays as his late ones. Both in *Richard II* and *Antony and Cleopatra*, scene after scene passes with no exact indication of where we may be. With Cleopatra we are surely in Egypt, with Cæsar in Rome. Pompey appears, and the talk tells us that both Egypt and Rome are elsewhere; but positively where Pompey is at the moment we never learn.[1] Indoors or outdoors? The action of the scene or the clothing of the characters will tell us all we need know. But, suddenly transported to the Parthian war, our whereabouts is made amply plain. It is, however, made plain by allusion. The information peeps out through talk of kindred things; we are hardly aware we are being told, and, again, we learn no more than we need to learn. This, truly, is a striking development from the plump and plain

> Barkloughly Castle call they this at hand?

of *Richard II*, even from the more suggestive

> I am a stranger here in Gloucestershire,
> These high wild hills and rough, uneven ways
> Draws out our miles . . .

by which Shakespeare pictures and localises the manœuvres of Richard and Bolingbroke when he wants to. But the purpose is the same, and the

[1] Unless it may be said that we learn in the scene after whereabouts he *was*.

method essentially the same. Towards the end of
the later play come scene after scene of the march-
ing and counter-marching of armies, of fighting,
of truce, all the happenings of a two-days' battle.
Acts III and IV contain twenty-eight scenes long
and short; some of them are very short; three of
them have but four lines apiece. The editors
conscientiously ticket them "A plain near Actium"
"Another part of the plain" "Another part of
the plain" and so on, and conclude that Shakespeare is really going too far and too fast, is indeed
(I quote Sir Edmund Chambers) " in some danger
of outrunning the apprehension of his auditory."
Indeed he might be if this cinematographic view
of his intentions were the right one! But it utterly
falsifies them. Show an audience such a succes-
sion of painted scenes—if you could at the pace
required—and they would give attention to nothing
else whatever; the drama would pass unnoticed.
Had Shakespeare tried to define the whereabouts of
every scene in any but the baldest phrases—the
protesting editors seem not to see that he makes
no attempt to; only *they* do!—he would have had
to lengthen and complicate them ; had he written
a labelling line or two he would still have distracted
his audience from the essential drama. Ignoring
whereabouts, letting it at most transpire when it
naturally will, the characters capture all attention.
This is normally the great gain of the unlocalised
stage; no precious words need be wasted, nor
ingenuity spent, in complying with the undramatic
demands of space and time; incarnation of
character can be all in all. Given such a crisis
as this the gain is yet greater. We are carried
through the phases of the two-days' battle; and

what other stage convention would allow us so varied a view of it, would so isolate the true drama of it? For do we not pass through such a crisis in reality with just that indifference to time and place? These scenes, in their kind, show Shakespeare's stagecraft, not at its most reckless, but at its very best, and exemplify perfectly the freedom he enjoyed that the stage of visual illusion has inevitably lost. His drama is attached solely to its actors and their acting; that, perhaps, puts it in a phrase. They carry place and time with them as they move. The modern theatre still accepts the convention that measures time more or less by a play's convenience; a half-hour stands for an hour or more, and we never question the vagary. It was no more strange to an Elizabethan audience to see a street in Rome turning to the Senate House by the drawing of a curtain and the disclosure of Cæsar's state, to find Cleopatra's monument now on the upper stage because Antony had to be drawn up to it, later on the lower because Cleopatra's death scene could best be played there; it would seem that they were not too astonished even when Juliet, having taken leave of Romeo on the balcony of her bedroom and watched him descend to the lower stage, a few lines later, the scene continuing, came down to the lower stage herself, bringing, so to speak, her bedroom with her—for this apparently is what she must have done.[1] For neither Senate House, monument nor balcony had rights and reality of their own. They existed for the convenience of the actors,

---

[1] I fancy, though, that the later Shakespeare would have thought this a clumsy device.

whose touch gave them life, a shadowy life at most; neglected, they existed no longer.[1]

Shakespeare's stagecraft concentrates, and inevitably, upon opportunity for the actor. We think now of the plays themselves; their first public knew them by their acting; and the development of the actor's art from the agilities and funniments of the clown, and from formal repetition or round-mouthed rhetoric to imaginative interpreting of character by such standards as Hamlet set up for his players, was a factor in the drama's triumph that we now too often ignore. Shakespeare himself, intent more and more upon plucking out the heart of the human mystery, stimulated his actors to a poignancy and intimacy of emotional expression—still can stimulate them to it, as no other playwright has quite learnt to do.

THE SPEAKING OF THE VERSE

His verse was, of course, his chief means to this emotional expression; and when it comes to staging the plays, the speaking of the verse must be the foundation of all study. Three hundred years have put difficulties in our way here; though there are some besides—as one imagines—of Shakespeare's own making. Surely his syntax must now and then have puzzled even his contemporaries. Could they have made much more than we can of Leontes'

---

[1] How far this is true of other dramatists than Shakespeare I do not pretend to say; nor how far, with him, the influence of the private theatre, making undoubtedly towards the scenic stage and (much later) for illusion, did not modify his practice, when he had that stage to consider. A question, again, for the bibliographers and historians.

Affection! thy intention stabs the centre;
Thou dost make possible things not so held,
Communicat'st with dreams;—How can this be?
With what's unreal thou coactive art,
And fellow'st nothing; Then, 'tis very credent
Thou may'st co-join with something; and thou dost;
And that beyond commission; and I find it,
And that to the infection of my brains,
And hardening of my brows.

The confusion of thought and language is dramatically justified. Shakespeare is picturing a genuinely jealous man (the sort of man that Othello was *not*) in the grip of a mental epilepsy. We parse the passage and dispute its sense; spoken, as it was meant to be, in a choking torrent of passion, probably a modicum of sense slipped through, and its first hearers did not find it a mere rigmarole. But we are apt to miss even that much. Other passages, of early and late writing, must always have had as much sound as sense to them; but now, to the casual hearer, they convey more sound than sense by far. Nor do puns mean to us what they meant to the Elizabethans, delighting in their language for its own sake. Juliet's tragic fantasia upon ' Ay ' and ' I ' sounds all but ridiculous, and one sympathises with an actress hesitating to venture on it. How far, apart from the shifting of accents and the recolouring of vowels, has not the whole habit of English speech changed in these three hundred years? In the theatre it was slowing down, one fancies, throughout the eighteenth century ; and in the nineteenth, as far as Shakespeare was concerned, it grew slower and slower, till on occasions one thought—even hoped—that shortly the actor would stop altogether. There may have been more than one cause; imitation of the French Augustans, the effort to make antiquated phrases understood, the increasing size of the theatres themselves would all contribute to it. The result, in any case, is disastrous. Elizabethan drama was built upon vigour and beauty of speech. The groundlings may often have deserved Shakespeare's strictures, but they would stand in discomfort for an hour or so to be stirred by the sound of verse. Some of the actors no doubt were robustious periwig-pated fellows, but, equally, it was no empty ideal of acting he put into Hamlet's mouth—and Burbage's. We may suppose that at its best the mere speaking of the plays was a very brilliant thing, comparable to *bel canto*, or to a pianist's virtuosity. The emotional appeal of our modern music was in it, and it could be tested by ears trained to the rich and delicate fretwork of the music of that day. Most Hamlets—not being playwrights—make a mild joke of telling us they'd as lief the town-crier spoke their lines, but we may hear in it the echo of some of Shakespeare's sorest trials.

The speaking of his verse must be studied, of course, in relation to the verse's own development. The actor must not attack its supple complexities in *Antony and Cleopatra* and *Cymbeline*, the mysterious dynamics of *Macbeth*, the nobilities of *Othello*, its final pastoral simplicities in *A Winter's Tale* and *The Tempest* without preliminary training in the lyricism, the swift brilliance and the masculine clarity of the earlier plays. A modern actor, alas, thinks it simple enough to make his way, splay-footed, through

The cloud-capped towers, the gorgeous palaces . . .

though Berowne's

I, forsooth, in love . . .

or one of Oberon's apostrophes will defeat him utterly. And, without an ear trained to the delicacy of the earlier work his hearers, for their part, will never know how shamefully he is betraying the superb ease of the later. If we are to make Shakespeare our own again we must all be put to a little trouble about it. We must recapture as far as may be his lost meanings; the sense of a phrase we can recapture, though instinctive emotional response to it may be a loss for ever. The tunes that he writes to, the whole great art of his music-making, we can master. Actors can train their ears and tongues and can train our ears to it. We talk of lost arts. No art is ever lost while the means to it survive. Our faculties rust by disuse and by misuse are coarsened, but they quickly recover delight in a beautiful thing. Here, at any rate, is the touchstone by which all interpreting of Shakespeare the playwright must first—and last—be tried.

THE BOY-ACTRESS

More than one of the conditions of his theatre made this medium of accomplished speech of such worth to him. Boys played the women parts; and what could a boy bring to Juliet, Rosalind or Cleopatra beyond grace of manner and charm of speech? We have been used to women on the stage for two hundred and fifty years or more, and a boy Juliet—if the name on the programme revealed one, for nothing else might—would seem an odd fish to us; no one would risk a squeaking Cleopatra; though, as for Rosalind, through three-parts of the play a boy would have the best of it. But the parts were written for boys; not, therefore, without consideration of how boys could act them most convincingly. Hence, of course, the popularity of the heroine so disguised. The disguise was perfect; the make-believe one degree more complex, certainly, than it needs to be with us; but once you start make-believe it matters little how far you go with it; there is, indeed, some enjoyment in the make-believe itself. But, further, it is Shakespeare's constant care to demand nothing of a boy-actress that might turn to unseemliness or ridicule. He had not much taste for what is called 'domestic drama,' nor does he dose us very heavily with Doll Tearsheet, Mistress Overdone and their like. Constance mourns Arthur's loss, Lady Macduff has her little son, but no mother croons over the child in her arms. Paulina brings Hermione's baby to Leontes, it is true; but see with what tact, from this point of view, the episode is managed. And love scenes are most carefully contrived. Romeo and Juliet are seldom alone together; never for long, but in the balcony scene; and in this, the most famous of love scenes, they are kept from all contact with each other. Consider *Antony and Cleopatra*. Here is a tragedy of sex without one single scene of sexual appeal. That aspect of Cleopatra is reflected for us in talk about her; mainly by Enobarbus, who is not mealy-mouthed ; but his famed description of her voluptuousness is given us when she has been out of our sight for several scenes. The play opens with her parting from Antony, and in their two short encounters we see her swaying him by wit, malice, and with the moods of her mind. Not till the story takes its tragic plunge and sex is drowned in deeper passion are they ever intimately together; till he is brought to her dying there has been occasion for but one embrace. Contrast this with a Cleopatra planned to the advantage of the actress of to-day.

Shakespeare, artist that he was, turned this limitation to account, made loss into a gain.[1] Feminine charm—of which the modern stage makes such capital—was a medium denied him. So his men and women encounter upon a plane where their relation is made rarer and intenser by poetry, or enfranchised in a humour which surpasses more primitive love-making. And thus, perhaps, he was helped to discover that the true stuff of tragedy and of the liveliest comedy lies beyond sensual bounds. His studies of women seem often to be begun from some spiritual paces beyond the point at which a modern dramatist leaves off. Curious that not a little of the praise lavished upon the beauty and truth of them—mainly by women—may be due to their having been written to be played by boys !

Much could be said for the restoring of the celibate stage; but the argument, one fears, would be academic. Here, though, is practical counsel. Let the usurping actress remember that her sex is a liability, not an asset. The dramatist of to-day may refuse to exploit its allurements, but may legitimately allow for the sympathetic effect of it; though the less he does so, perhaps, the better for his play and the more gratitude the better sort of actress

[1] There is no evidence, of course, that he felt it a loss, no such reference to the insufficiency of the boy-actress as there is to the over-self-sufficiency of the clown. Women did appear in the Masks, if only to dance, so the gulf to be bridged was not a broad one. But the Elizabethan was as shocked by the notion of women appearing upon the public stage as the Chinese playgoer is to-day.

will show him. But Shakespeare makes no such demands, has left no blank spaces for her to fill with her charm. He asks instead for self-forgetful clarity of perception, and for a sensitive, spirited, athletic beauty of speech and conduct, which will leave prettiness and its lures at a loss, and the crudities of more Circean appeal looking very crude indeed.

THE SOLILOQUY

This convention of the boy-actress may be said to give a certain remoteness to a play's acting. The soliloquy brings a compensating intimacy, and its use was an important part of Shakespeare's stagecraft. Its recognised usefulness was for the disclosing of the plot, but he soon improved upon this. Soliloquy becomes the means by which he brings us not only to a knowledge of the more secret thoughts of his characters, but into the closest emotional touch with them too. Here the platform stage helped him, as the stage of scenic illusion now defeats his purpose. But it is not altogether a question of ' realism ' and the supposed obligation this lays upon a real man in a real-looking room to do nothing he would not do if the whole affair were real.

There is no escape from convention in the theatre, and all conventions can be made acceptable, though they cannot all be used indiscriminately, for they are founded in the physical conditions of the stage of their origin and are often interdependent one with another. Together they form a code, and they are as a treaty made with the audience. No article of it is to be abrogated unless we can be persuaded to consent, and upon its basis we surrender our imaginations to the play-wright.

With the soliloquy upon the platform stage it is a case—as so often where convention is concerned—of extremes meeting. There is no illusion, so there is every illusion. Nothing very strange about this man, not even the dress he wears, leaning forward a little we could touch him; we are as intimate and familiar with him as it is possible to be. We agree to call him Hamlet, to suppose that he is where he says he is, we admit that he thinks aloud and in blank verse too. It is possible that the more we are asked to imagine the easier we find it to do. It is certain that, once our imagination is working, visual illusion will count for little in the stimulating of emotion beside this intimacy that allows the magnetism of personality full play.

There is no more important task for the producer of Shakespeare than to restore to the soliloquy its rightful place in a play's economy, and in particular to regain for it full emotional effect. We now accept the convention frigidly, the actor manœuvres with it timidly. Banished behind footlights into that other world of illusion, the solitary self-communing figure rouses our curiosity at best. Yet further adapted to the self-contained methods of modern acting, the soliloquy has quite inevitably become a slack link in the play's action, when it should be a recurring reinforcement to its strength. Shakespeare never pinned so many dramatic fortunes to a merely utilitarian device. Time and again he may be feeling his way through a scene for a grip on his audience, and it is the soliloquy ending it that

will give him—and his actor—the stranglehold.
When he wishes to quicken the pulse of the action,
to screw up its tension in a second or so, the soliloquy serves him well. For a parallel to its full
effectiveness on Shakespeare's stage we should
really look to the modern music-hall comedian
getting on terms with his audience. We may
measure the response to Burbage's

O, that this too too solid flesh would melt . . .

by recalling—those of us that happily can—Dan
Leno as a washerwoman, confiding domestic
troubles to a theatre full of friends, and taken
unhindered to their hearts. The problem is not
really a difficult one. If we solve the physical
side of it by restoring, in essentials, the relation
between actor and audience that the platform stage
provided, the rest should soon solve itself.

COSTUME

The problem of costume, when it arises, is a
subtler one; nor probably is it capable of any
logical solution. Half the plays can be quite
appropriately dressed in the costume of Shakespeare's own time. It is a false logic which
suggests that to match their first staging we should
dress them in the costume of ours. For with
costume goes custom and manners—or the lack
of them. It may be both a purge and a tonic
to the sluggish-fancied spectator to be shown a
Prince of Denmark in coat and trousers and a
grave-digger in a bowler hat, for reminder that
here is a play, not a collection of ritualised quota-
tions. But physic is for the sick; also, there may
be less drastic cures. When archæology took hold

upon the nineteenth-century mind it became a matter of moment to lodge Hamlet in historic surroundings; and withers were wrung by the anachronisms of ducats and a murder of Gonzago, French rapiers and the rest. A needless teasing difficulty; why reproduce it in terms of a young man in a dinner jacket searching for a sword—a thing not likely to be lying about in his mother's sitting-room—with which to kill Polonius, who certainly has window curtains to hide behind instead of arras? This gain of intimacy—with a Hamlet we might find sitting opposite at a dinner-party—may well be a gain in sympathy. It was originally a great gain, a precious gift to Shakespeare's audience. But we pay too high a price for it.

What was the actual Elizabethan practice in this matter of costuming is not comprehensively known. We can only say safely that, as with other matters, it was neither constant, consistent, nor, from our present point of view, rational. It was based upon the use of the clothes of the time; but these might be freely and fantastically adapted to suit a particular play or advantage some character in it. Dramatic effect was probably the first consideration and the last. There were such fancy dresses as Oberon or Puck or Caliban might wear; there was always the symbolising of royalty, and a king would wear a crown whenever he could; there was the utility of knowing Romans from Britons by sight in *Cymbeline*, the martial Roman from the effete Egyptian in *Antony and Cleopatra*, and a Scottish lord when you saw him in *Macbeth*, if we may judge by Malcolm's comment upon Rosse's appearance:

My countryman; and yet I know him not.

Our difficulty, of course, arises mainly over the historical plays. Not over the English Histories, even so; we can dress Richard III or Henry V by the light of our own superior knowledge of what they wore, and never find it clash violently with anything Shakespeare has put on their backs or in their mouths. But when we come to Julius Cæsar plucking open his doublet, to the conspirators against him with their hats about their ears, and to Cleopatra's

> Cut my lace, Charmian.

not to mention British Imogen in her doublet and hose, we must stop and consider.

The common practice is, in these instances, to ignore the details of Shakespeare's text altogether; to dress Cæsar in his toga, Cleopatra in her habit as she lived, with never a stay-lace about her (though, truly, the costumier, let alone, will tend to get his fashion a few thousand years wrong and turn her out more like the wife of Tut-ankhamen); and as to Imogen and her surroundings, we do our best to compromise with skins and woad. This may be a lesser evil than presenting a Cæsar recalling Sir Walter Raleigh and a Cleopatra who would make us think of Mary Queen of Scots, but it is no solution of the problem. For the actors have to speak these lines, and if action and appearance contradict them, credibility is destroyed. And the constant credibility of the actor must be a producer's first care. Nor is this all, nor is it, perhaps, the most important thing to consider. The plays are full of reference, direct and indirect, to Elizabethan custom. They are, further, impregnated with what we call Renaissance feeling, some more, some less, but all to a degree. Now of this last we have a sense which is likelier to be a better help to their appreciation than any new-fangled knowledge of the correct cut of Cleopatra's clothes will be! We know Iago for a Macchiavellian figure (so called), and miss none of Shakespeare's intention. But if ever two men breathed the air of a sixteenth-century Court, Hamlet and Claudius of Denmark do, and to relate them in habit and behaviour to the twilight figures of Saxo Grammaticus is as much a misinterpretation as any mauling of the text can be. They exist essentially doubtless— as do all the major characters of the plays—in their perennial humanity. But never let us forget the means by which this deeper truth of them is made vivid and actual. There have been better intellects than Shakespeare's, and poetry as good as his. He holds his supreme place by his dramatist's necessary power of bringing thought and vague emotion to the terms of action and convincing speech; further, and far more than is allowed, by his peculiar gift of bringing into contribution the commonplace traffic of life. However wide the spoken word may range, there must be the actor, anchored to the stage. However high, then, with Shakespeare, the thought or emotion may soar, we shall always find the transcendental set in the familiar. He keeps this balance constantly adjusted; and, at his play's greatest moments, when he must make most sure of our response, he will employ the simplest means. The higher arguments of the plays are thus kept always within range, and their rooted humanity blossoms in a fertile upspringing of expressive little things. Neglect or misinterpret these, the inner wealth of Shakespeare will remain.

no doubt, and we may mine for it, but we shall have levelled his landscape bare.

Shakespeare's own attitude in this matter of costume and customs was as inconsistent as his practice was casual. He knew what his Cæsar or Cleopatra would be wearing and dropped in a reference to it without a thought. Yet the great Romans were aliens to him, though the great idea of Rome fired his imagination. So Brutus, Cassius and Antony are not turned to typical Elizabethan gentlemen; to the end of that play he is striving to translate Plutarch. Whenever, on the other hand, even for a moment he has made a character all his own, he cannot but clothe it in lively familiar detail. And Cleopatra's are the coquetries of a great lady of his own time, in their phrasing, in their savour. When the heights of the tragedy have to be scaled, manners will not so much matter. But make her, at the play's beginning, a pseudo-classic, languishing Oriental, and you must do it in spite of Shakespeare, not by his help. What then is the solution of this problem, if the sight of the serpent of old Nile in a farthingale will too dreadfully offend us? We can compromise. Look at Tintoretto's and Paolo Veronese's paintings of classic subjects. We accept them with calm.

Sometimes, within the boundaries of a play, the centuries seem all at odds. *Cymbeline* need not trouble us, its Roman Britain is pure ' once upon a time.' But in *King Lear*, for instance, Shakespeare is at unwonted pains to throw us back into some heathen past. Yet Edmund is another Iago, Edgar might have been at Wittenberg with Hamlet, and Oswald steps straight from the seventeenth-century London streets. Here, though, the dominant barbarism is the important thing; the setting for Goneril and Regan, Lear's tyranny and madness, and Gloucester's blinding. To a seventeenth-century audience Oswald was so identifiable a figure that it would not matter greatly how he dressed; the modern designer of costume must show him up as best he may. Each play, in fine, if it presents a problem at all, presents its own.

THE INTEGRITY OF THE TEXT

The text, one says at first blush, can present no problem at all. The plays should be acted as Shakespeare wrote them—how dispute it? They should be; and it is as well, before we discuss hard cases, to have the principle freely admitted. Lip-service enough is done it now-a-days, and Colley Cibber's *Richard III*, Tate's *Lear* and Garrick's improvements are at the back of our bookshelves, but we still find Messrs. John Doe and Richard Roe slicing out lines by the dozen and even a scene or so, or chopping and changing them to suit their scenery. This will not do. Shakespeare was not a perfect playwright; there can be no such thing. Nor did he aim at a mechanical perfection, but at vitality, and this he achieved. At best then, we cut and carve the body of a play to its peril. It may be robustly, but it may be very delicately organised. And we still know little enough of the laws of its existence, and some of us, perhaps, are not such very skilful surgeons; nor is any surgeon to be recommended who operates for his own convenience.

This good rule laid down, what are the exceptions that go to prove it? There is the pornographic difficulty. This is not such a stumbling-block to us as it was to Bowdler, to some bright young eyes now-a-days it is quite unobservable, in fact. Yet, saving their presence, it exists; for it exists æsthetically. Shakespeare's characters often make obscene jokes. The manners of his time permitted it. The public manners of ours still do not; we demand, at least, a certain obliquity. Now the dramatic value of a joke is to be measured by its effect upon an audience, and each is meant to make its own sort of effect. If then, instead of giving them a passing moment's amusement, it makes a thousand people uncomfortable and for the next five minutes very self-conscious, it fails of its true effect. This argument must not be stretched to cover the silliness of turning ' God ' into ' Heaven ' and of making Othello call Desdemona a ' wanton ' (the practice, as I recollect, of the eighteen-nineties), nor to such deodorising of *Measure for Measure* that it becomes hard to discover what all the fuss is about. If an audience cannot think of Angelo and the Duke, Pompey and Lucio, Isabella and Mistress Overdone, and themselves to boot, as fellow-creatures all, the play is not for them. Othello must call Desdemona a whore, and let those that do not like it leave the theatre; what have such queasy minds to do with the pity and terror of her murder and his death? Again, to make Beatrice so mealy-mouthed that she may not tell us how the devil is to meet her at the gates of hell, " like an old cuckold with horns on his head," is to dress her in a crinoline, not a farthingale. But suppression of a few of the more scabrous jokes will not leave a play much the poorer; nor, one may add, will the average playgoer be much the wiser or merrier for hearing them, since they are often quite hard to understand.

Topical passages are a similar difficulty. With their savour, if not their very meaning lost, they show like dead wood in the living tree of the dialogue and are better, one would suppose, cut away. But no hard-and-fast rule will apply. Macbeth's porter's farmer and equivocator will never win spontaneous laughter again. But we cannot away with them, or nothing is left of the porter. Still the baffled low comedian must not, as his wont is, obscure the lines with bibulous antics. There will be that little dead spot in the play, and nothing can be done about it. Rosencrantz' reference to the " aery of children " is meaningless except to the student. Is the play the poorer for the loss of it? But the logic that will take this out had better not rob us of

> Dead shepherd, now I find thy saw of might;
> Who ever loved that loved not at first sight?

And there is the strange case of

The lady of the Strachy married the yeoman of the wardrobe.

Nobody knows what it means, but everybody finds it funny when it is spoken in its place. And this has its parallels.

In general, however, better play the plays as we find them. The blue pencil is a dangerous weapon; and its use grows on a man, for it solves too many little difficulties far too easily.

Lastly, for a golden rule, whether staging or costuming or cutting is in question, and a com-

prehensive creed, a producer might well pin this
on his wall: Gain Shakespeare's effects by Shakespeare's means when you can; for, obviously, this
will be the better way. But gain Shakespeare's
effects; and it is your business to discern them.

LOVE'S LABOUR'S LOST

H ERE is a fashionable play; now, by three hundred years, out of fashion. Nor did it ever, one supposes, make a very wide appeal. It abounds in jokes for the elect. Were you not numbered among them you laughed, for safety, in the likeliest places. A year or two later the elect themselves might be hard put to it to remember what the joke was.

THE PRODUCER'S PROBLEM

Were this all one could say of *Love's Labour's Lost*, the question of its staging to-day—with which we are first and last concerned—would be quickly answered, and Lose no Labour here be the soundest advice. For spontaneous enjoyment is the life of the theatre. If a performance must be accompanied by a lecture, if, for instance, when Holofernes is at the point of

Bone, bone for benè: Priscian a little scratched. 'Twill serve,

we need his modern exemplar in cap and gown, standing on one side the proscenium, to interrupt with " One moment, please! The allusion here, if you wish to appreciate its humour, is to . . ."; or if he must warn us, " In the next scene, ladies and gentlemen, you will notice a reference to the charge-house on the top of the mountain. This is thought by the best authorities to denote . . ." not much fun will survive. For a glossary in the programme something might be said, even for a preliminary lecture. No; this last, one fears, would leave the actors with too hard a task turning class-room back to theatre. Half-digested information lies a little heavily on one's sense of humour.

It is true that with no play three hundred years old can we press our 'spontaneous' too hard. For the full appreciation of anything in Shakespeare some knowledge is asked of its why and wherefore. Hamlet and Falstaff however, Rosalind and Imogen, are compact of qualities which fashion cannot change; the barriers of dramatic convention, strange habit, tricks of speech are of small enough account with them. But what is back of these word-gymnastics of Rosaline and Berowne, Holofernes' jargon, Armado's antics? The play is a satire, a comedy of affectations. The gymnastics, the jargon and the antics are the fun. Yet a play hardly lives by such brilliancies alone. While the humour of them is fresh and holds our attention, actors may lend it a semblance of life; for there they are, alive in their kind! No play, certainly, can count on survival if it strikes no deeper root nor bears more perennial flowers. If its topical brilliance were all, Shakespeare's name tagged to this one would keep it a place on the scholar's dissecting table; in the theatre *Love's Labour's Lost* would be dead, past all question. But there is life in it. The satire beside, Shakespeare the poet had his fling. It abounds in beauties of fancy and phrase, as beautiful to-day as ever. We find in it Shakespeare the dramatist learning his art. To students the most interesting thing about the play is the evidence of this; of the trial and error, his discovery of fruit-

2

ful soil and fruitless. The producer, pledged to present an audience with a complete something, cannot, of course, be content with promise and experiment. Measuring this early Shakespeare by the later, we may as well own there is not much more. But the root of the matter is already in him; he is the dramatist born, and all, or nearly all, is at least instinct with dramatic life. It is oftenest his calculations and his cleverness that betray him.

For satire and no more is too apt to prove dramatically fruitless. A play's values are human values, and a playwright's first task is to give his creatures being. Imaginative love for them may help him to; even hate may; but a mocking detachment cannot. If he is to shoot at their follies he must yet build up the target first; and if it is not a convincing one there will be little credit in the shooting. He cannot, of course, in a play, take direct aim himself, unless he use the method of the Moralities or its like. There is the less direct method of twisting a set of familiar heroic figures awry. Shakespeare made this experiment, not too successfully, in *Troilus and Cressida*. But his obvious plan will be to turn one or more of his creatures satirists themselves, and under their cover plant his own shafts. Even so, he must give the victims their chance, or the play will be lopsided and come tumbling down.

The Shakespeare that sets out to write *Love's Labour's Lost* is a very clever young man, a wit, a sonneteer. He is ' in the movement.' He flatters his admirers by excelling in the things they admire; he will flatter his rivals hardly less by this attention

3

he means to pay them. But your clever young
man is usually more than a little impressed by the
things he mocks at; he mocks at them in self-
defence, it may be, lest they impress him too
much. Mockery is apt, indeed, to capitulate to
the thing mocked, to be absorbed by it. And these
academic follies of Navarre, the fantastic folly of
Armado, the pedantic folly of schoolmaster and
parson—sometimes the satire is so fine that the
folly seems the clever young man's own. Yet this
weakness of the would-be satirist is the budding
dramatist's strength. Shakespeare cannot resist
his creatures; he never quite learned to. He
cannot make mere targets of them. He cannot
resist his own genius, poetic or dramatic; all
through the play we find the leaven of it working.
He has not written ten lines before the poet in
him breaks bounds. Is this the voice of that frigid
wiseacre Navarre; does this suggest the 'little
academe '?

> Therefore, brave conquerors—for so you are,
> That war against your own affections
> And the huge army of the world's desires.

But the clever young man recollects himself; and
here, soon enough, is the sort of thing he has set
out to write.

King. How well he's read, to reason against reading!
Dumain. Proceeded well, to stop all good proceeding!
Longaville. He weeds the corn, and still lets grow the
weeding.
Berowne. The spring is near, when green geese are
a-breeding.
Dumain. How follows that?
Berowne. Fit in his place and time.
Dumain. In reason nothing.
Berowne. Something then in rhyme.

4

Pretty tricksy stuff! Well enough done to show that he quite enjoyed doing it, but the sort of thing that almost anyone could learn to do. No signpost on the road to *Hamlet*, certainly.

But mark the dramatist in his provision at the outset of the conflict and balance that every play needs, in the setting of Berowne against his companions, one man's common-sense against the crowding affectations (a sporting conflict), an ounce of reality for counterweight to a ton of shams (an instructive balance). Here also, for the moralist-critic, is the play's moral issue defined at the outset; but let us not suppose Shakespeare to have been oppressed by this. Despite his present-day idolaters he was probably not high-purposed from his cradle; moreover, he is likely to have gained most of his knowledge of life by writing plays about it. That is not a provocative paradox, but a key to the mind and method of the artist. Time and again Shakespeare tells us that he sees the world as a stage. He would not think that a belittling comparison; he takes his art too seriously. Not portentously, but as simply seriously as any man will take his purpose in life when he is lucky enough to be sure of it. We all need some centre of experience to argue from, if the world beyond our experience is to have any meaning for us. The artist transforms and multiplies experience by imagination, and may even come to think that what is true of his art will be true of the world it mirrors. This sounds absurd. But life does seem to be governed by surprisingly simple laws; and human beings, wherever and whatever they may be, do not greatly differ in essentials. That is the working hypothesis upon which art and religion, and

5

imaginative genius in general, proceed. And let it be said of the theatre that a very short time in it will teach one what fine clothes and fine manners may amount to. The theatre was for Shakespeare a laboratory where he worked—if but in a mimic sense—with human material. His method, his means to enlightenment, was to take a story and put the worth of it, its truth to nature, to the test of personal expression. The story might suffer; if it was not true to nature, it generally would. But Shakespeare was, on the whole, a most unconscientious story-teller, except when history bound him. Sometimes he would make a sacrifice to symmetry, as when, in *Measure for Measure*, he marries Isabella to the Duke; but he may have felt this to be poetic justice upon such a morally consistent lady. The story may be burked, neglected or finished off anyhow, as in *Much Ado About Nothing*, *Twelfth Night* and *As You Like it*. It may hang at the heels of the chief character, as in *Hamlet*. What men are, in fact, comes to concern him far more than what they do. Already in this pretty play of *Love's Labour's Lost* it instinctively concerns him, though not even doing but mere clever talk is his ostensible concern. And when he passes to the giant theme of *King Lear*, to the sweep of historic vision that is in *Antony and Cleopatra*, stretching his medium of expression till it seems to crack and break, he concerns himself, even then, with little which cannot be rendered into human passion, human pity—which cannot, in fact, be put to this laboratory test. He—literally—has no use for theories and abstract ideas. He is neither philosopher nor moralist, except as he must seem to be, making his creatures one or the other.

6

He is a playwright; he projects character in action, and with the truth of the one to the other his power and responsibility end. If this is the playwright's limitation, it is also his strength; for to this test of human response—not mimic, truly, but real; yet the mimic but reflects the real—all philosophy and morality must finally be put.

In this earliest essay, then, we may divine the dramatist to be; and we find dramatist putting wit and poet to the proof. Shakespeare will have set out to do his best by his creatures one and all; but while Berowne grows under his hand into a figure, finally, of some dramatic stature, while the Princess, simple, straightforward, shrewd, is made flesh and blood, in the speaking of seven lines, Navarre, though a natural focus of attention and discussing himself unsparingly, remains a bundle of phrases, and Dumain and Longaville have about the substance of echoes. Of the humbler folk; Costard for three-quarters of the play is the stage Fool, but suddenly, when he comes to the acting of his Worthy, we have :

Costard. I Pompey am, Pompey surnam'd the big—
Dumain. The great.
Costard. It is great, sir; Pompey surnam'd the great;
That oft in field, with targe and shield, did make my foe to sweat;
And travelling along this coast, I here am come by chance,
And lay my arms before the legs of this sweet lass of France.
If your ladyship would say " Thanks, Pompey," I had done.
Princess. Great thanks, great Pompey.
Costard. 'Tis not so much worth; but I hope I was perfect: I made a little fault in " great."

And these two last lines have, mysteriously and unexpectedly, given us the man beneath the jester. Then, with another thirty words or so, Costard (and Costard's creator) settles Sir Nathaniel the Curate, till now little but a figure of fun, snugly in our affections.

> There, an't shall please you; a foolish mild man; an honest man, look you, and soon dashed! He is a marvellous good neighbour, in sooth; and a very good bowler: but, for Alisander, alas, you see how 'tis;—a little o'erparted.

And settles himself there the more snugly in the doing it! Throughout the play, but especially towards the end, we find such outcroppings of pure dramatic gold.

Drama, as Shakespeare will come to write it, is, first and last, the projection of character in action; and devices for doing this, simple and complex, must make up three-quarters of its artistry. We can watch his early discovery that dialogue is waste matter unless it works to this end; that wit, epigram, sentiment are like paper and sticks in a fireplace, the flaring and crackling counting for nothing if the fire itself won't light, if these creatures in whose mouths the wit is sounded won't 'come alive.' To the last he kept his youthful delight in a pun; and he would write an occasional passage of word-music with a minimum of meaning to it (but of maximum emotional value, it will be found, to the character that has to speak it). His development of verse to dramatic use is a study in itself. He never ceased to develop it, but for a while the dramatist had a hard time with the lyric poet. The early plays abound, besides, in elaborate embroidery of language done for its own sake.

8

This was a fashionable literary exercise and Shakespeare was an adept at it. To many young poets of the time their language was a new-found wonder; its very handling gave them pleasure. The amazing things it could be made to do! He had to discover that they were not much to his purpose; but it is not easy to stop doing what you do so well. Yet even in this play we may note the difference between the Berowne of

> Light seeking light doth light of light beguile;
> So ere you find where light in darkness lies
> Your light grows dark by losing of your eyes!

and of the soliloquy beginning

> And I forsooth in love . . .[1]

Turn also from one of the many sets of wit to Katharine's haunting answer when Rosaline twits her with rebellion against Cupid:

Rosaline. You'll ne'er be friends with him; he kill'd your sister.
Katharine. He made her melancholy, sad, and heavy:
And so she died: had she been light, like you,
Of such a merry, nimble, stirring spirit,
She might have been a grandam ere she died;
And so may you, for a light heart lives long.

Compare it with the set of wit that follows.

Rosaline. What's your dark meaning, mouse, of this light word?
Katharine. A light condition in a beauty dark.
Rosaline. We need more light to find your meaning out.
Katharine. You'll mar the light, by taking it in snuff;
Therefore I'll darkly end the argument.

---

[1] Which, says Dr. Dover Wilson, belongs to the play's revising. But this does not invalidate my point; rather the contrary.

But Rosaline won't let her, and they manage to get five more rather spicier exchanges. It is all very charming; the mere sound is charming, and a 'set of wit' describes it well. Get a knowledge of the game and it may be as attractive to watch for a little as are a few sets of tennis. But pages on pages of such smart repartee will not tell us as much of the speakers as those few simple lines of Katharine's tell us—of herself and her love for her sister, and of Rosaline too.

The play sets out, as we said, to be a flattering satire upon such humours, and the playwright must set up before he pulls down, break before he satirises; and the two processes do, doubtless, get mixed. Can we detect a Shakespeare impatient, for a moment, with his pleasant task? He has punned and joked his best.

> *Berowne.* White-handed mistress, one sweet word with thee.
> *Princess.* Honey, and milk and sugar; there is three.
> *Berowne.* Nay then, two treys, (an if you grow so nice)
> Metheglin, wort and malmsey—Well run, dice!

Nor will he neglect the ever-satisfying humours of cuckoldry.

> *Katharine.* Veal, quoth the Dutchman:—is not veal a calf?
> *Longaville.* A calf, fair lady?
> *Katharine.* No, a fair lord calf.
> *Longaville.* Let's part the word.
> *Katharine.* No, I'll not be your half;
> Take all and wean it; it may prove an ox.
> *Longaville.* Look, how you butt yourself in these sharp mocks!
> Will you give horns, chaste lady? do not so.
> *Katharine.* Then die a calf, before your horns do grow.

It amused him, no doubt, as it amused his audience; it is just too well done to have been done mechanically. But when, of a sudden, the Princess breaks out with

> Are these the breed of wits so wondered at?

may we not hear for the moment his voice sounding through hers? For it is a barren business finally, and his fecund spirit could not long be subdued to it. With but little violence we could twist the play into a parable of his own dramatic progress. Even as Berowne at its end forswears

> Taffeta phrases, silken terms precise,
> Three-pile hyperboles, spruce affectation,
> Figures pedantical . . .

so might Shakespeare be swearing to pass from them himself on towards the prose of *As You Like It* and the strong verse of *Julius Cæsar*. A notion not to be taken too seriously, perhaps. But a few years hence he is to let Hamlet record a taste for plays set down with as much modesty as cunning, with

> . . . no sallets in the lines to make the matter savoury, nor no matter in the phrase that might indict the author of affectation; but . . . an honest method, as wholesome as sweet and by very much more handsome than fine.

And certainly there are signs that, whether he knew it or no, the leaven was already working beneath this bright wit, this delight in words and their rhythm and melody, that was soon to turn a pretty speechifying Mercutio into the stark man of

> A plague of both your houses!
> They have made worms' meat of me:
> I have it and soundly too . . .

and the word-spinning Romeo into that doomed taciturn figure of

> Is it ev'n so? Then I defy you, stars.

The dramatist was in the making who was to fashion a Falstaff out of the old pickpurse of Gadshill, who was to pitch on the preposterous tale of *The Merchant of Venice*, and charge it (triumphantly, yet all but disastrously) with the passion of Shylock.[1]

But the producer must consider carefully just what the carrying power of this more embryonic drama is, and how he can effectively interpret to a modern audience the large remainder of the play. What fresh life can his actors give to this fribble of talk and nice fantasy of behaviour? As satire it means nothing to us now. Where are the prototypes of these cavaliers and ladies—of Armado and Holofernes, Moth and Nathaniel the Curate? We can at best cultivate an historical sense of them. There remains the verse, and the pretty moving picture of the action. Our spontaneous enjoyment will hang upon pleasant sounds and sights alone, sense and purpose apart. Really, it almost amounts to this! Better face the difficulty at its worst. Is there any surmounting it?

THE METHOD OF THE ACTING

If only the last act were in question we should not need, I think, to qualify our Yes; for this is throughout as much mask as play, it is meant to

---

[1] He pitched, we may say, upon two preposterous tales, and redeemed the second by the romantic beauty of Portia.

charm us as much by sight and sound as by story
and character. To take one passage:

Rosaline.   What would these strangers?   Know their minds,
        Boyet.
        If they do speak our language, 'tis our will
        That some plain man recount their purposes:
        Know what they would.
Boyet.   What would you with the princess?
Biron.   Nothing but peace and gentle visitation.
Rosaline.   What would they, say they?
Boyet.   Nothing but peace and gentle visitation.
Rosaline.   Why, that they have, and bid them to be gone.
Boyet.   She says, you have it, and you may be gone.
King.   Say to her we have measured many miles
        To tread a measure with you on the grass.
Boyet.   They say that they have measured many a mile
        To tread a measure with you on this grass.
Rosaline.   It is not so.   Ask them how many inches
        Is in one mile: if they have measured many,
        The measure then of one is easily told.
Boyet.   If to come hither you have measured miles,
        And many miles, the princess bids you tell
        How many inches do fill up one mile.
Berowne.   Tell her we measure them by weary steps.
Boyet.   She hears herself.

The action is implicit enough. Boyet must move,
to the rhythm of the verse, between one group and
the other. He bids fair to tread out a mile himself
if the game last much longer. But the two groups
draw together after this, and then break into
couples. In a moment the music starts. Instead
of dancing, however, we have a dance of dialogue.
The couples circle the stage to the sound of the
music, speaking their lines as they pass through
the arc the audience commands. Finally, Boyet,
who can have held his place in the centre, steps
forward as chorus; and for comment, full to the
audience:

The tongues of mocking wenches are as keen
As is the razor's edge invisible,
Cutting a smaller hair than may be seen;
Above the sense of sense; so sensible
Seemeth their conference; their conceits have wings,
Fleeter than arrows, wind, thought, swifter things.

The music stops. Four lines more, and the scene is over.

Now this has no dramatic value, properly so called. It hardly furthers such plot as the play has; unless to make a tangle to be disentangled a scene later without more consequence can be called the furthering of a plot. It does not develop character. The dialogue is mere mischief. There is, of course, the satire; its edge is blunted by time. But if the music is clear and fine, as Elizabethan music was, if the costumes strike their note of fantastic beauty, if, above all, the speech and movements of the actors are fine and rhythmical too, then this quaint medley of mask and play can still be made delightful. But it asks for style in the acting. The whole play, first and last, demands style. A vexingly indefinable thing, a hackneyed abracadabra of a word! One should apologise for bringing it into such a practical discussion as this pretends to be. Nor will the play as a whole, perhaps, be so entirely susceptible to its magic. But the theatre must deal in magic sometimes.

The conjecture that *Love's Labour's Lost* was first written for the delectation of a coterie of magnificent young men has been capped by the conjecture that some of them may have acted in it at the time. As custodians of the culture of the age, sponsors to this reborn mirroring art of the drama, they might well have recognised that they, in their own persons, apparel and conversation, mirrored and witnessed to that culture supremely. And they might, just for once, have condescended! They would have been cast, of course, for Navarre, Berowne, Dumain and Longaville. Some senior-junior might have been found to fit Boyet, and someone who would modestly prefer himself to Monsieur Marcade. Whether there is much historical likelihood in the suggestion I do not know. If so, the other parts would be played, we may suppose, by professionals. There are the mask and the antic (the anti-mask) in the last act; and we know that in the great Court shows the lords and ladies did the graceful dancing and left the grotesque to trained tumblers and dancers. One would like to complete the picture by imagin-ing the Princess and her ladies played by some of those Maids of Honour, who used on occasion to " friske and hey about." Would not that Mistress Fitton who—most historically—tucked up her skirts and, cloaked like a man, marched out of Whitehall to meet her lover, have been ready for once to play the boy and act the woman? It could further be argued that the dialogue for Navarre and his lords is of just such stuff as those young bloods of culture delighted to try their wits and tongues at; and that there is not much more in it, nothing emotional (except for Berowne; and his most emotional outburst is counted a later addition, when the play was perhaps being revised for the public stage), no impersonation, nothing that demands the professional actor with his greater comic or rhetorical force. Navarre and his lords are, in modern stage slang, ' walking gentlemen '; but they need to walk magnificently and to talk with a fine assurance. The historical question is not pertinent to our present discussion, but these implications of it are. Whoever acted the play, it must have been in these respects exquisitely done, or it could not have endured its two hours' traffic, though its every joke made a topical hit. Happy-go-lucky, with the hope of a few guffaws for punctuation, could never have been a method for this sort of thing. The audience, too, must have been attuned to its fantasies, to its exquisite passions. How passionate the Elizabethans were! They were capable—those that were articulate and responsive at all—of intellectual passion, as Englishmen have hardly been since. And when poetry and rhetoric display it in the charged atmosphere of the theatre, the effect— even the distant echo of it—is intense. Navarre and his

> . . . little academe
> Still and contemplative in living art

are oath-bound fanatics ; Berowne's gibing is but at the futility and hypocrisy of their professions.

> Warble, child—make passionate my sense of hearing,

says Armado, who is their caricature. Holofernes, that passionate latinist, Sir Nathaniel ridiculously emulating him, little Moth, with his piping and strutting, an incarnate mockery of them all, Costard reflecting their features in grimaces, their fine phrases in nonsense, the most reverberate things sounding hollow under the thwack of his bauble—all these, then, in accent and motion must be keyed to a sort of ecstasy, to a strange surpassing of this modern work-a-day world, if the play is to be anything at all but a sonata thumped out on a dumb piano, a picture painted by the colour-blind. A hard task for the actor; doubly hard, in that he must key up his audience too. For by time and subject it is all three hundred years strange to us. We need an interpretation of absolute value; and that is a contradiction in terms. We must have a beauty of speech that will leave us a little indifferent to the sense of the thing spoken. Navarre and his friends and their ladies must show such distinction and grace that we ask no more pleasure in their company. Armado and the rest must command us by the very skill with which they remake mankind. It must indeed all be (to quote Berowne) if it is to exist at all,

. . . as the style shall give us cause to climb in the merriness.

THE STAGING, COSTUME AND CASTING

The play will profit little by any departure from Shakespeare's own staging; nor is this, in its simplicity, hard to deduce. A designer may shift the period of costume fifty years or so back—or forward for that matter—if his taste dictate, and no great harm done. A certain grace may be added to Navarre and his friends by dressing them French fashion, or Italian. The Englishman was not famous for his taste in dress; though, if Portia may be trusted, he only made matters worse when he picked up notions abroad, his doublet in Italy, his round hose in France, his bonnet in Germany and his behaviour everywhere. But these scrupulous young men would be purists in tailoring too. And a comedy of affectations, of nice phrases, asks that its characters should be expressive to their boot-toes, significant in the very curl of a feather. None of the others are hard to picture. Shakespeare sets Armado before us clearly, the refined traveller from tawny Spain, dignified and mock melancholy, carrying his rapier as might a conqueror of kingdoms, though for ' remuneration ' to his messengers he cannot exceed three farthings, and must go shirtless, woolward for penance; he is black suited, of course. Figure of fun as he is, though, his pride is not pinchbeck, nor must he look merely ridiculous. He sponges on no one, and hides his poverty all he can. When Costard infamonizes him among potentates—and the potentates, we may be sure, die with laughing— Shakespeare gives him great dignity in humiliation. We can picture Moth, that well-educated infant. Navarre, we may suppose, has made him page to the tall angular Spaniard for the fun of the contrast in the looks of them. Moth knows this well enough, be sure; and just how to make the best of his own share in the composition. He should not dress like Armado, that would coarsen the joke. He might still be wearing the King's livery. So might Costard, who makes a third in this conjunction, and has a flavour of Sancho Panza about him, even as Armado every now and then sets one thinking of that greater Don, yet in the womb of imagination. To complete this group we have the harsh, drab aspect of Holofernes; Sir Nathaniel, sober-suited but well-liking; and Dull, who is dull of countenance and clothing too. These will stand in sombre contrast to the choicegarmented Court and the rainbow beauty of the Princess and her ladies; till, for their show of the Nine Worthies, they too burst into flower, and into most wondrous and gaudy flowering.

The pictorial values in the pageantry of this last scene have their dramatic value too. The Russian maskings have been laid aside, cumbrously fantastic things, convenient cloakings. Yesterday Navarre and his friends were recluse philosophers; splendid even so, no doubt, but with a pallid splendour. To-day they are in love and glowingly apparelled, in which symbolism their ladies can match them; and against this delicately blended colouring the village pageant tells crude and loud. Into the midst there suddenly steps Marcade, in black from head to foot. He hardly needs to speak.

> The king your father—
> Dead, for my life!
> Even so, my tale is told.

Berowne takes order.

> Worthies, away! The scene begins to cloud.

And it must seem to cloud; the gay colours fading out, the finery folding about its wearers like wings. But this is not the end, for the end must not be melancholy. The country-folk have yet to sing and dance their antic; a little crowd of them, dressed to match the

> . . . daisies pied and violets blue,
> And lady-smocks all silver white,
> And cuckoo-buds of yellow hue . . .

The comedy of affectations comes to its full close upon notes of pastoral freshness and simplicity.

19

As with costume so with scene; we shall gain nothing, we shall indeed be the worse for surrendering the freedoms of Shakespeare's stage. If we insist on placing and picturing the play's action now definitely here, now exactly there, we shall only be making complex what he has left simple, and find ourselves set to answer riddles which he never asked. The convention of place involved is ' about Navarre's Court '; outdoors, it seems to be, nothing more definite. The recluse King and his courtiers may walk there, the Princess may be met there, and no vows be broken; a pricket may be driven near for shooting, a pageant be shown there, a measure trod on the grass. Armado and his page walk there; so do the parson and the schoolmaster, unquestioned. Closer definition than this will be troublesome. The place, in fact, is not a place at all, within the modern scenic meaning. If we needs must paint the picture, it will need to be generalised, atmospheric, symbolic; the problem for a designer is quite a pretty one. Shakespeare, we may notice, hardly makes full practical demand upon the resources of the public theatre of the time. No use is made of the inner stage, though this might have served well for the Princess's pavilion. But the line

Whip to our tents as roes run o'er the land

suggests a further flight. Except for one episode the play asks no more than a bare stage with a couple of openings to it, just such a provision as would be found in that great hall where we may suspect it was first acted. The scene of the philosophers' mutual discovery that they are, all four of them, forsworn and in love calls, however,

20

for three hiding-places, of which one must be aloft; for Berowne says :

> Like a demi-god here sit I in the sky.

But no harder mechanical problem faces the producer.[1]

This convention of place, and a similar freedom with time, encourages a very different method of construction from that proper to the theatre we

[1] And at this point in the play, also at this particular point in the scene, Dr. Dover Wilson scents revision. It may well be that Berowne, like the King and Longaville, originally hid on the stage level. But the stagecraft as we have it is worth examination. When Berowne is aloft Dumain does not come into his view till some minutes after Longaville espies him. This suggests that, if and when the play was revised for a public theatre, the tree (of some editors) to be climbed was no more than the gallery at the back of the stage, though a property tree might have been set against it, so that he would appear to be in its branches. Isolated property trees that can be climbed must be very solid affairs indeed. Berowne knows of Longaville's approach, for the King names him. But Longaville's only warning of Dumain's is " Company! Stay! " Then he bolts to hiding, not having himself seen, perhaps, who the intruder is. This is likely, for Shakespeare was from the beginning too good a dramatist to duplicate an effect. It would seem as if the stage stayed apparently empty for a moment, while Berowne said:

> All hid, all hid; an old infant play.

Next that Dumain entered, walking slowly down to the accompaniment of

> Like a demi-god here sit I in the sky
> And wretched fool's secrets heedfully o'er-eye.

At which point Berowne sees his back:

> More sacks to the mill!

Then identifies him:

> O heavens, I have my wish!
> Dumain transform'd: four woodcocks in a dish!

With all the emphasis on *four*, a climax well worked up !

know to-day, in which place, and even time, are positive and definite things. The dramatist, so set free, thinks more of his characters and less of their surroundings; he can manœuvre them, absolved from such conformity, in the varied world of their own humours and passions. Elizabethan dramatic form has greater flexibility than ours; this, with its vehicle of verse (a further, more potent enfranchisement) gives it an emotional range which the modern dramatist must seek to compass by quite other means, by thrift of expression and tension sustained, by many hard economies. The scenic articulation of Shakespeare's later plays is masterly. They may seem loose-jointed, they are really supple and strong, delicate occasionally, never to be hacked at with impunity. *Love's Labour's Lost* is put together very simply; a little clumsily here and there, but alongside simplicity a little clumsiness will pass muster. The main device—an obvious escape from monotony—is the alternating of one group of characters with the other, and of verse scenes with prose. The blending of the two groups at the last is as obvious a conclusion. But in the contriving of the changes we find him feeling his way—now missing it, now forcing it, truly—to incidental dramatic advantage. A simplicity and elasticity of form was always to suit him best; it gave full play to his power of developing character.

We come quickly to a petty crudity of construction, of which a later Shakespeare might not have been guilty; it is amusing to note how conventional editing, covering the fault, makes it worse. Berowne, at the King's behest, departs, with Costard in charge, to seek Armado. But close upon his heels Armado appears. The editors mark a change of scene. Some shift the locality; some are for 'Scene 2, the same.' The shift of locality supposes, of course, a regard for its realities which Shakespeare never had; but 'Scene 2, the same' suggests an interval of time which is the last thing a swift-moving comedy requires at its outset. Let us see how Shakespeare himself gets over the difficulty he creates. He wants to divide two scenes of comedy by a scene of caricature. He does not think of localities. Berowne and Costard are to leave the stage in search of Armado. Armado is to appear a second later upon that same stage. This is clumsy, it will seem resourceless; it will affect his audience as a false note in music would, or a trip in a dance. Therefore he has Berowne leave the stage first, lets Costard lag behind for a little solitary funniment, and then bolt after Berowne. If the funniment raises a laugh, that breaks contact, as it were, and continuity. The bolting breaks the rhythm of movement: it also brisks up the end of the scene [1] and provides a contrast to the slow, stately entrance of Armado. All of which, together with the curiosity the new-comer to the play arouses, will make us forget the incongruity and will compensate for the clumsiness. Shakespeare, of course, did not need to reason this out. His dramatic instinct served him; so would anyone's. Act the little passage as it is set down and its effect will be automatic. A pity to comment upon it! But these innocencies of drama must be protected against

[1] One cannot be always defining the sense in which one is using this word; the context, one hopes, will make it plain. Here, of course, it implies a division of dialogue.

23

reasoning men; the more innocent they are the more protection they seem to need.

The rest of the play's comings and goings, by which its action is spaced and divided, look likely enough, if we do not insist upon looking at them through distorting spectacles. They have not much other dramatic value. If we want to make main divisions the play can be made to fall well enough into three parts. The Quarto (as usual) runs it through at a stretch; the Folio (as usual) divides it into five acts. If four pauses are to mean four intervals of distraction, this is a large allowance for so slight a play. I should myself prefer the two, which would leave Acts I and II of the Folio as a unit of exposition; Acts III and IV for the uninterrupted working out of the simple plot; and Act V (which is longer than either of the other two put together) for pageantry. This arrangement happens to exhibit some consistency in time. The first part will mark the occasion—to all intent the day—of the Princess's arrival; the second fills the following morning; the third—Holofernes and Sir Nathaniel having dined presumably at midday—the afternoon following this.[1] But a producer might do well to abide by the Quarto. It would at least compel him to keep the acting brisk. The whole play could be put through in less than two hours.

The Folio's Act IV does show, perhaps, a more complex significance of structure; there

[1] There are some signs of confusion in Act III, Sc. i. Berowne (and possibly at the moment Shakespeare) seems to think the Princess is coming to hunt in the afternoon. As it happens, she comes in the morning, only a minute or two after Berowne himself has started for his ride.

is what looks like a deliberate use of the hunting subject as a link between scene and scene. It is as if Shakespeare wanted to lead on—despite the variety and incongruity of the action here—without a marked break to the dominatingly important scene of the sonnet reading and the four woodcocks in a dish. No disturbing climax, at any rate, intervenes between Berowne's soliloquy (which closes the third act) and this scene, which is the climax properly evolved from it and the climax of the play besides. How far this is deliberate, how far instinctive, may be profitless speculation; the producer should undoubtedly observe the effect.[1]

But the best of the play's craft is lodged in the dialogue; in its twists and turns, in the shifts of

[1] Hence he should not tolerate an interval, even if he allow a pause, after the Folio's Act III.

The scene following the soliloquy, after recording Berowne's distracted spurring of his horse up-hill (the audience can easily tell that it was he, if he has just been before them, booted and spurred, whip in hand), goes practically straight to the hunting subject. This is returned to for a finish by means of a shout within (which, I believe, should rather be 'shoot' within) and Costard's running out with a halloo. The next scene begins,

> Very reverend sport truly,

and ends with

> Away! the gentles are at their game;

while Berowne begins the scene following with

> The king he is hunting the deer.

Conventionalised time is used, of course, throughout the four scenes. This, moreover, is all we hear of the day's hunting. But it is enough for Shakespeare. A hunt is toward; and no more excuse is needed in an English countryside or an English theatre—nor would be in the most categorical of plays —for anyone and everyone to turn up incontinently.

25

time and key, which are stage directions of the clearest sort. We have the brisking of a scene's end by such a piece of cross-fire as

Boyet. Do you hear, my mad wenches?
Margaret. No.
Boyet. What then, do you see?
Rosaline. Ay, our way to be gone.
Boyet. You are too hard for me.

The author of *Twelfth Night* might have thought this a little crude; but it serves its purpose.

We find another hint to the actors to ' work up an exit,' as the cant phrase has it, at the end of the scene of preparation for the pageant of the Nine Worthies. Dull, having spoken not a word nor understood one neither, yet offers to make one in a dance and to play the tabor. Holofernes —no dancer, we presume!—turns down the offer with contempt. He departs. Armado has taken precedence of him and bidden him follow, so he departs pretty testily. But if Dull, left last, does not show us in a dozen steps what a chance they are missing—Shakespeare did not know the comedian's craft! And Shakespeare, both to his joy and sorrow, did!

Half the dramatic meaning of a passage may lie in the action it suggests.

Armado. Is not lead a metal heavy, dull and slow?
Moth. Minime, honest master, or rather, master, no.
Armado. I say lead is slow.
Moth. You are too swift to say so:
Is that lead slow which is fired from a gun?
Armado. Sweet smoke of rhetoric!
He reputes me a cannon; and the bullet, that's he;
I shoot thee at the swain.
Moth. Thump, then, and I flee.

26

We must picture the long black barrel of a man, slow-gaited even in talk, and the little page, daintily at fence with him, and then off the stage at a bound. The art of it is akin to the artifice of a ballet.

The actor, in fine, must think of the dialogue in terms of music; of the tune and rhythm of it as at one with the sense—sometimes outbidding the sense—in telling him what to do and how to do it, in telling him, indeed, what to *be*. By the sense and sound together of the very first words spoken Shakespeare is apt to make a character clear to actor and audience both.

> Boy, what sign is it when a man of great spirit grows melancholy?

Who, after the ample measure and high tone of that, could mistake Armado? See, again, his taciturn, self-conscious, amorous condescension and the wench Jaquenetta's mumchance allurement —the comic likeness and contrast of the two—hit out for us in a duet just forty-five words long.

> Maid.
> Man.
> I will visit thee at the lodge.
> That's hereby.
> I know where it is situate.
> Lord, how wise you are!
> I will tell thee wonders.
> With that face?
> I love thee.
> So I heard you say.
> And so, farewell.
> Fair weather after you

—though, alas, Jaquenetta's country phrases have lost half their flavour for us now.

Shakespeare seems in the main content with the

obvious contrast which the two groups and the shifts from verse to prose and back to verse again afford him. Prose is first brought into the play naturally enough by Costard and Dull and the reading of Armado's letter. The constricted pedantry of Armado's soliloquy ending the first act is followed pat—if no interval is allowed—by the strongest, simplest blank verse we have had yet. This effect is definitely dramatic, as of a sudden breeze of common-sense blowing in. Berowne, it is true, has been preaching to us from this pulpit, but all tangled up himself in pun and antithesis. Even with the Princess and the ladies, however, we are back thirty lines later at

> The only soil of his fair virtue's gloss,
> If virtue's gloss will stain with any soil,
> Is a sharp wit match'd with too blunt a will,

at

> The young Dumain, a well-accomplish'd youth,
> Of all that virtue love for virtue lov'd . . .

and the like. Shakespeare's dramatic instinct has prompted the change ; his art does not sustain it. He is still too occupied with the actual writing of the play, with himself, in fact, and his own achievements, to spare to his characters that superabundant strength which can let them seem to develop a life of their own. He relapses, therefore, to the thing he has learnt how to do ; as a man may find every new tune he whistles turning, despite him, into that one old tune he knows. He is still a little tangled—to make the point again—as his own Berowne is, in the affectations he is out to satirise.

But Berowne is the play's truly dynamic figure,

and he and Shakespeare struggle out of the toils together. His

And I forsooth in love . . .

lifts the play into living comedy. It is his comic ecstasy that gives life to the scene planned as the play's climax, when all four men discover that they are all four in love. The rest of it is mere liveliness of wit and humour, and as arbitrary as a practical joke. The King, Longaville and Dumain are as much frigid phrase-makers in love as ever they were out of it. Shakespeare has still a last act to write, it may be argued. He must not anticipate the promise to woo

In russet yeas and honest kersey noes.

But we shall not find him in the flush of his genius missing one chance because another must be waited for and hanging up a character's development. If characters are only to be moved by a series of jerks from one rigidity to the next, they will be more suitably played by marionettes than men. Man as marionette will be amusing for one scene, for a second less so ; we shall find as much interest in a third look at him as in a look at any other stage furniture. And when we do reach the last act, Shakespeare, it seems, can make no more of his King, Longaville and Dumain in the end than he could at the beginning. There is no life in the fellows, and that's all about it. This lack of dramatic life, then, from which, let us own, the larger part of the play, and its more purposed part, suffers, its producer must face. It is, five-sixths of it, more decorative exercise than drama. It must

29

therefore be given, as near as may be, what we have called an absolute value in sight and sound.

In yet one more respect the play may suffer by its transference from the Elizabethan stage. The acting of women by boys was in itself a contribution to these absolute values. Further, if we do not allow for the effect of this stringency upon Shakespeare's stagecraft even at its most mature, we shall be constantly at fault. Not that he seems to have felt it a drawback; among all his sideglances at actors and acting we find, I think, no hint that it irks him. It did not impoverish his imagination nor lead, on the whole, to any undue suppression of the womanly side in his plays. It may influence his choice of subject; he does not trouble with domestic drama. Without doubt it determines what he will and will not ask woman characters and boy actors to do. Their love scenes are never embarrassing. They do not nurse babies. They seldom weep. He puts them, in fact, whenever he can, upon terms of equality with men; and women have been critically quick ever since to appreciate the compliment, not well aware, perhaps, how it comes to be paid them. For those conflicts of character which are the very life of drama he appoints weapons that each sex can wield with equal address; insight and humour, a quick wit and a shrewd tongue—the woman's the shrewder, indeed; in compensation, is it, for the softer advantages, the appealing charm, that his celibate theatre denied them? Out of a loss he plucks a gain. Release from such reality drew him to set the relation of his men and women upon the plane of the imagination. It asked from the boy actors a skill, and a quite impersonal beauty of speech and conduct; those absolute qualities, in fact, of which we speak. The Elizabethan theatre lacked many refinements, but at least its work was not clogged nor its artistry obscured by the crude appeal of sex, from which the theatre to-day is perhaps not wholly free. No one wants to banish women from the stage; and it might not be an easy thing to do. But actresses may well be asked to remember what their predecessors achieved, and by what means.

In *Love's Labour's Lost*, however, the Princess and the ladies are not, and cannot be made, much more than mouthpieces for wit and good sense. As to love-making, the Princess gives us the cue with

> We have received your letters, full of love;
> Your favours, the ambassadors of love;
> And, in our maiden council, rated them
> At courtship, pleasant jest, and courtesy,
> As bombast, and as lining to the time:
> But more devout than this, in our respects,
> Have we not been; and therefore met your loves
> In their own fashion, like a merriment.

It is all to be gallant, open and above-board.

> Saint Cupid, then! and, soldiers, to the field.

They are to be leagued encounters; and no two of the lovers are ever alone. But how few of Shakespeare's love scenes now or later need it embarrass anyone to overhear! In more than one sense he wrote for daylight effect upon an open stage. Passion and tragedy and high romance he has still to deal with; he has still to find out how to write Juliet and Isabella, Desdemona, Cleopatra. But already the problem of Portia and Beatrice

31

is solved, and Rosalind can be heard telling Orlando:

> You shall never take her without her answer unless you take her without her tongue.

THE TEXT, AND THE QUESTION OF CUTTING IT

The text presents practical difficulties, and one is fortunate to have Dr. Dover Wilson's fresh work upon it in the new *Cambridge Shakespeare*. A flaw or so in method or result there may be; to set about correcting them with his own tools one would need uncommon skill. But it will be worth while to test his conclusions by their effect —as far as we can divine it—upon the play's staging, for good or ill. This is, in fact, the ultimate test to which many of these bibliographical subtleties must submit.

The pronouncement upon two imperfectly cancelled passages in Act IV, Scene iii, and Act V, Scene ii, answers to this test well. Some repetition in the first passage is patent; and, given a blue pencil and told to consider the dramatic upbuilding of the speech, who could make any other cut than that between lines 292 and 315? The textual muddle in the second is as obvious; and if Dr. Dover Wilson's solution of it (though here certainly he but follows other editors) needs a stage-manager's support, it can be had for the sake of Berowne's

> Studies my lady? mistress, look on me.

For the dramatic intention is unmistakable. The King and Princess have made their exchanges,

32

important and effective ones. If Berowne's and Rosaline's follow close, the importance of theirs must be lessened, unless some violent contrast is achieved, boisterous and quite out of key. But by the simple device of keeping these two chief characters still and silent while Dumain and Katharine, Margaret and Longaville say their say —it must not be too long a say, nor important enough to demand our entire attention—we are put on the alert, held in suspense, brought to be wondering whatever will occur when the silence between them is broken. And an actual silence, a pause—no actor could help making one—must occur before

> Studies my lady? . . .

Thereafter, without effort or undue emphasis, or any illiberal self-assertion, Rosaline and Berowne, as they are meant to, top the scene.

This passage surely shows re-drafting, and evidence of Shakespeare's more practised hand. But do the alterations run quite on Dr. Dover Wilson's lines? Would Dumain begin, " *But* what to me . . ." unless a previous speech had begun, " *And* what to me, my love? " It is unlikely that Shakespeare would ever have let the love-affairs even of two less important couples lapse in silence. May not Berowne's

> A twelvemonth! Well, befall what will befall . . .

originally have followed upon Margaret's

> The liker you; few taller are so young . . .?

And why, here and elsewhere, does Dr. Dover Wilson bring in evidence the possible size of

4

Shakespeare's writing-paper and the number of lines he could write on it? It was a scarcer substance with him, no doubt, than it is with his commentators. To suppose, though, that having taken a piece on which to write a new passage he could not stop till he had filled it. . . ! But Dr. Dover Wilson *cannot* suppose this.

Another point of consequence is the Rosaline-Katharine confusion in Act II, Scene i. The suggested elucidation is best studied in the new *Cambridge Shakespeare* itself. It is as good as a detective story. Really, Scotland Yard should turn sometimes to our scientific bibliographers! Is one graceless to make any question of a verdict reached by such ingenuity? By the practical, dramatic test it stands, in the main. It is only that these nice investigations have the defects of their qualities; they tend to prove too much.

The case for this transference of the masks and the mistaken identity motive from Act II, Scene i, to Act V is, of course, strong upon several grounds. But to conclude from this, as Dr. Dover Wilson does, that Shakespeare, making the alteration, meant to leave the earlier scene practically naked of everything but a dialogue between the King and the Princess, and a little questioning of Boyet by the young men and a little chaff for the young ladies, is to brand him as a very slack craftsman indeed. First, it is well-nigh inconceivable that he can let this scene pass, Rosaline and Berowne both present, and deny them an encounter. (Besides, without the first of the two passages between them, or something in its place, how is the King to read his letter?) The dialogue was originally written for Rosaline to play masked, no doubt. Later, Shakespeare did not care to change it; there was no compelling reason he should. She could just as well hold up her travelling mask at Berowne's approach to tantalise him and fog him in his patronising recognition of her. We must remember the space convention of the Elizabethan stage; the distance across it was anything in reason. Cannot we see him stalking the lady? And a mask in those days was a woman's accustomed protection in more senses than one.

The scene's second encounter between the two, however, is redundant in itself, and of no constructional use; it is, indeed, an impediment to the action. Berowne and his fellows would not hang long behind when the King had departed; the Elizabethans appreciated ceremony in the theatre and out of it. But the stage, with its doors at the back, allowed for a many-paced exit. The three courtiers could follow with due observance if the questions to Boyet began promptly; hardly otherwise. The redundancy, a certain clumsiness of construction, and, not least, the extreme artificiality of this ' set of wit' suggest it as part of an earlier growth, which, for some reason, was not clearly cut away. In its continuance, too, the dialogue shows every sign of having been hacked about. For instance,

> Good sir, be not offended:
> She is an heir of Falconbridge,

is halt, if not maimed.

So much, then, for the test of stage effect. But (before we pass on) among Dr. Dover Wilson's own tests, are speech-headings such a safe guide to

revision as he makes out? These are not, for
the dramatist, a part of his play. Shakespeare,
let us say, has a character in his head called
Ferdinand, King of Navarre. If he wrote the
play containing it at a sitting he might—though
it is by no means inevitable—begin with one
speech-heading and go on using it till the end.
But it is likely enough that having made it ' Ferd: '
on Monday and spent Tuesday at work upon
Armado, on Wednesday he may be putting ' King '
and on Friday ' Nav: ' and even by the Monday
following be using ' King ' ' Nav:' ' Ferd: '
whichever comes first from his pen. He does not
give a thought—why should he?—to such an
entirely irrelevant matter. It will be the same
with stage directions. While he is waiting for a
scene to take fire in his mind, he may write with
careful elaboration: " Enter the Princess of
France with three attending ladies and three
lords," even as a schoolboy hopefully heads his
paper with a copperplate ' Composition.' But
when he sits down to it all-fired, " Enter the
ladies " is good enough. Then he can get to
work.

No doubt there are clues to be picked from these
confusions that will not prove loose-ended. But
when the critical editor begins " A natural and
reasonable way of explaining . . ." one's con-
currence is apt to be checked, even unfairly, by
the over-riding thought that what is reasonable
to a critic is not therefore natural to a playwright.

We now come to the question of the permissible
cutting of the text for modern performance,
and no play in the canon presents greater diffi-

culties. The principle is plain. A producer must take his stand with the first Cambridge editors and Garrick (Garrick! he may well exclaim) and resolve to "lose no drop of the immortal man." Still, no one need let his principles befool him. We need hardly hold sacred all that the printer has left us. The redundant passages in Act IV, Scene iii, and Act V, Scene ii, may go; Shakespeare's final intention is plain as a pikestaff.[1] There are besides a few sentences that are hopelessly corrupt; these we need not make a fuss about. But there are far more than a few that are nowadays almost, if not quite, incomprehensible, that require, at any rate, a professor and a blackboard as first aid. And over these principle and common-sense come to loggerheads. For common-sense does seem to urge: the average man in an audience will either understand these things or he won't; if he won't, cut them. The problem, however, is not quite so simple as this. If there is life in a play we cannot cut even ounces of flesh from it with impunity. If it is an articulated whole we cannot remove a joint and a sinew or two and not risk laming it. Thirty lines may be thirty lines and no more; but they may be—and they should be—an organic part of a scene.

For instance: Moth and Costard enter to Armado.

Moth. A wonder, master; here's a Costard broken in a shin.

Armado. Some enigma, some riddle: come,—thy *l'envoy*; begin.

Costard. No egma, no riddle, no *l'envoy*; no salve in the

---

[1] It is the present redundancy, of course, that we keep.

mail, sir. O! sir, plantain, a plain plantain; no *l'envoy*, no *l'envoy*: no salve, sir, but a plantain.

Armado. By virtue, thou enforcest laughter; thy silly thought, my spleen; the heaving of my lungs provokes me to ridiculous smiling: O! pardon me, my stars. Doth the inconsiderate take salve for *l'envoy*, and the word *l'envoy* for a salve?

Moth. Do the wise think them other? Is not *l'envoy* a salve?

Armado. No, page: it is an epilogue or discourse, to make plain
    Some obscure precedence that hath tofore been sain.
I will example it:
    The fox, the ape, and the humble-bee,
    Were still at odds, being but three.
There's the moral: Now the *l'envoy*.

Moth. I will add the *l'envoy*; say the moral again.

Armado. The fox, the ape, and the humble-bee,
    Were still at odds, being but three.

Moth. Until the goose came out of the door,
    And stay'd the odds by adding four.
Now will I begin your moral, and do you follow with my *l'envoy*.
    The fox, the ape, and the humble-bee,
    Were still at odds, being but three:

Armado. Until the goose came out of door,
    Staying the odds by adding four.

Moth. A good *l'envoy*, ending in the goose; would you desire more?

Costard. The boy hath sold him a bargain, a goose, that's flat:—
    Sir, your pennyworth is good, an your goose be fat.
    To sell a bargain well is as cunning as fast and loose:
    Let me see a fat *l'envoy*; ay, that's a fat goose.

Armado. Come hither, come hither: How did this argument begin?

Moth. By saying that a costard was broken in a shin.
    Then call'd you for the *l'envoy*.

Costard. True, and I for a plantain; thus came your argument in:

Then the boy's fat *l'envoy*, the goose that you bought.
And he ended the market.

Armado. But tell me; how was there a costard broken in a shin?

Moth. I will tell you sensibly.

Costard. Thou hast no feeling of it, Moth: I will speak that *l'envoy*:

> I, Costard, running out, that was safely within,
> Fell over the threshold, and broke my shin.

Armado. We will talk no more of this matter.

Which last line alone we might expect an audience to appreciate!

What is a producer to do? How much of the stuff can any modern audience be brought to understand—even to understand, enjoyment apart? A glossary in the programme could give us first aid towards Moth's not very brilliant joke about Costard and shin, remind us that talk of a plantain leaf made the Elizabethans merry, even as a cry for brown paper and vinegar could once raise a laugh in Victorian farce—and a glossary will be needed for this very soon. But what can be done to recover such foundered word-play as

> No egma, no riddle, no *l'envoy*, no salve in the mail, sir,

or to give life and sense to Moth's

> Is not *l'envoy* a salve?

When we come to

> The fox, the ape, and the humble-bee,

we can, grown desperate, find Folio authority for a cut. The new Cambridge editors insist that it is an obviously topical joke, its application long

39

lost; we might get rid of it upon that ground.[1] But,—worse and worse!—we next come to elaborate jesting about a goose and a market.

Should a producer expunge the whole thing and bring Costard on to hear at once of his enfranchisement? This may well be the lesser evil. But one cannot thus eviscerate a scene and expect to see no wound. Here is an effect gained by the resolving of the long Armado-Moth duet into a trio, by rounding off the sententious folly and nimble mockery with the crude humour of the clown. The dialogue passes from prose to rhymed couplets; then becomes gay with jingle, which Costard jollily burlesques in that long lolloping metre. We must think of it all in terms of music, of contrasts in tone and tune, rhythm and breaking of rhythm. There is the value of the picture too, set before us and held for its minute or two; of the egregious dignity of Armado, Moth delicately poised, and Costard square-toed and cunning, not such a fool as he looks. All this has histrionic value, the sheer sense of the dialogue apart. Plots and character-schemes beside, all plays exist as schemes of sound, as shifting pictures, in decoration of thought and phrase, and the less their dependence on plot or conflict of character the more must they depend upon such means to beauty and charm. These 'set pieces' may be loosely and easily contrived, so that they still give that implicit

---

[1] But is this so? I can imagine an American editor three hundred years hence testing the verse which begins,

I never saw a purple cow . . .

for an allusion to President Wilson. Was not Roosevelt called a bull-moose? But the mere truth is that sixty million people or so once thought that funny in itself.

illusion of life which is the end of all drama; and we must never be made over-conscious of them, or the charm will vanish, even though the beauty remain. But in this play, as we have seen, much depends on them. We are, indeed, never very far from the actual formalities of song and dance. The long last act is half mask and half play; and in song and dance the play ends.

Therefore, though pretty picture and pleasant sound alone will never suffice, before sentence is passed on a difficult passage it might well be put upon some probation. Let the actors see what they can make of it by adroit movement and the nice turning of a phrase. There is danger here. Released from that troublesome obligation to make current sense of his goings-on—and he may well contend that it is a sin against nature for him to have to do so—the actor too readily turns acrobat; and the audience, doing their duty by Shakespeare, hardly expect to make much sense of the thing anyhow. Better cut half the play than act any of it on these terms; but better, then, not act it at all. There are passages, however (the one we have just quoted is not in its entirety one of them), which somehow do yield to such treatment. Who, with an ear for the music and rhythm of fine prose, will not take pleasure, for instance, in the very sound of

Armado. Go, tenderness of years! take this key, give enlargement to the swain, bring him festinately hither; I must employ him in a letter to my love.

Moth. Will you win your love with a French brawl?

Armado. How meanest thou? brawling in French?

Moth. No, my complete master; but to jig off a tune at the tongue's end, canary to it with your feet, humour it with turning up your eyes; and sigh a note and sing a note as if you swallowed love with singing love, sometime through the nose, as if you snuffed up love by smelling love; with your hat pent-house-like over the shop of your eyes; with your arms crossed on your thin belly-doublet like a rabbit on a spit: or your hands in your pockets, like a man after the old painting; and keep not too long in one tune, but a snip and away. These are complements, these are humours, these betray nice wenches that would be betrayed without these, and make them men of note—do you note me?—that are most affected to these.

Armado. How hast thou purchased this experience?

Moth. By my penny of observation.

Armado. But O—but O,——

Moth. The hobby horse is forgot.

Armado. Call'st thou my love hobby horse?

Moth. No, master; the hobby horse is but a colt—and your love perhaps a hackney. But have you forgot your love?

Armado. Almost I had.

Moth. Negligent student! learn her by heart.

Armado. By heart, and in heart, boy.

Moth. And out of heart, master: all those three I will prove.

Armado. What wilt thou prove?

Moth. A man, if I live: and this—by, in, and without, upon the instant. By heart you love her, because your heart cannot come by her; in heart you love her, because your heart is in love with her; and out of heart you love her, being out of heart that you cannot enjoy her.

It is pure *bravura*; it hangs up the action, it hardly develops character; Shakespeare the full-fledged dramatist would not have written it. We may indeed compare it to an *aria* in an opera. It calls for a comparable execution, an audience should get the same sort of pleasure from it. And if the musical value is not quite as great—well, we miss every word of the *aria* as a rule.

To make a tentative list of the passages with which nothing can be done, of the bits of dead wood, one may call them:

Armado. I love not to be crossed.
Moth. He speaks the mere contrary, crosses love not him.

Moth's line at least might come out. The joke can't be conveyed, nor is it worth the conveying.

The dancing horse is dead past resurrection. If a ruthless pencil does away with the lines that lead up to the point and the two that drop away from it, can the most fervid Shakespearean—more royalist than his king—complain?

The reference to the ballad of the King and the Beggar might go too. On the other hand, anyone who would mangle the discourse upon the four complexions, if it were only that he might so deprive us of Armado's

Define, define, well-educated infant,

is a butcher and botcher of texts.

The whole passage between Boyet, the ladies and Costard in Act IV, Scene i, which begins with the now cryptogrammatic pun,

Who is the suitor? who is the suitor?

—if one pronounces it sewtor the joke is lost, so it is to a modern audience if one calls it shooter—asks at first sight for drastic treatment. Say we surmount this first obstacle, eke out the everlasting jokes about cuckoldry that follow with a wink or two and a nod, we shall still be utterly lost in the tangle of talk—yet more equivocal in every sense—about archery and bowling. Nevertheless, if one is not to truncate the whole scene and end it with the Princess's departure—and this is structural alteration and inadmissible—

43

it may be better to go through with the gibberish, to let it seem so if it must. For again, consider the action, the lively picture; Boyet surrounded by the teasing girls, Costard ecstatic at the encounter! And are we to miss the little singing dance with which Rosaline takes leave? Apart from the charm of it—the girl and the gay old courtier answering and counter-stepping each other—and apart from the value of this little turmoil of rhythmic gaiety before we drop to our first experience of Holofernes and his pedantry, Shakespeare is bringing Rosaline by degrees to her due place of importance in the play, and no item of the process should be omitted.

As to Holofernes and Sir Nathaniel, it is a good part of the fun of them that neither the innocent Dull, nor we, can make out half the time what they are talking about. No need then, after all, to be troubled by

Priscian a little scratched,

or even by the mystery of the charge-house on the top of the mountain. But what can—what ever *can*!—be made of Moth's pleasantries about the five vowels and the horn-book (yet once again a cuckold's horn-book!) in the first scene of the last act? If ever a passage could serve in a competition with a prize given to the set of actors that extracted some legitimate effect from it, this could! Nor is it of any constructive conse- quence, nor does it add one stroke of character. Why not pass boldly, then, from Costard's achievement of

. . . honorificabilitudinitatibus: thou art easier swallowed than a flap-dragon.

to

Arts-man, preambulate,

and so to the play's business?

But really there is nothing more, save a line or two of obvious indecency easily left out, that the producer need wish to conjure away. There remains but to question one apparent corruption of text, which does obscure the action at an important point, then to point out one or two possible pitfalls in the casting of the parts, and this prefacing, grown longer than the play itself, may end.

The King, that noble gentleman and Armado's very good friend, having set on his butt to provide the entertainment of the Nine Worthies, encourages his guests in the doubtless far better entertainment of making outrageous fun of him. By the standards of the time this may not have seemed to be such very caddish behaviour. We recall the practical jokes played by the Duke and Duchess on Don Quixote. Cervantes could have commented, as Shakespeare cannot; but he let the business speak for itself. Still, it is possible that Shakespeare, young as he was and flattered, no doubt, by the approval of his own play's very select audience, had his private opinion upon this aspect of their gentility. Certainly, when the final trick is played on Armado, it is he, fantastic fool as he is, who shines out as the best gentleman amongst them, even as Don Quixote shone. The manner of the trick itself, however, is all confused in the text as we have it, and its matter is somewhat obscure. Berowne incites Costard to bring Armado's play-acting to utter grief by rushing on distraught with the sudden news that the wench Jaquenetta is cast away, is

two months gone, Armado the culprit. The
stage-directions that make this clear Dr. Dover
Wilson has most justly restored. And as justly
he restores to Armado the line that he must speak
to give point to the interruption:

> The party is gone.
>
> Fellow Hector, she *is* gone . . .

exclaims Costard. But the effect is still incomplete. The first line must surely be a part of
Hector the Worthy's speech (this Dr. Dover
Wilson does not hold). Where is the comic
incongruity of Costard's twist of the phrase otherwise? It is such an obvious trick; neither
Costard, nor Shakespeare, at this moment, could
neglect it. One suspects a pun in ' party.' It
can mean an antagonist, Achilles against Hector.
An intermediate line may be missing; it cannot be
restored unless someone should discover a colour-
able original of the pageant. But at least the
incident and its business can be rightly outlined
in action.

Further, it is surely clear—though to many
editors it does not seem to be—that in the accusa-
tion poor Armado *is* most scandalously ' in-
famonized.' Where would be the joke else?
The King and Princess, the courtiers and ladies
must, most of them, know by this time of his
ridiculous adoration of this country wench; and
we have seen how she treats him. Armado a
hypocrite! The whole character is destroyed at
a blow. If there were a guilty party, we might
rather suspect Costard, who did " confess the
wench." But it may all be a joke. Armado, at
least, is convinced so, for back he comes before

46

the play's end, quite his magnificently absurd self
again. And he, faithful among the faithless, will
be a votary still; but to philosophy no longer, to
the plough, to rusticity. We can imagine him,
though hardly a great success in the furrows behind
a team, sitting like Don Quixote beneath a tree—
again the comparison is irresistible—and piping
to the virginal Jaquenetta. Though, if Moth's
estimate of the young lady's character should,
after all, be the right one, Shakespeare is a finished
ironist already.

As to the casting of the comic parts; only with
Costard is it not plain sailing. Holofernes is
pedant incarnate, and Sir Nathaniel simple
parson. Jaquenetta is a country wench and
Dull is the village constable. But Costard, swain
though he is,[1] smacks both of Court-jester and stage-
clown. Shakespeare had often to make use of
these chartered comedians. Sometimes, as in
Twelfth Night, As You Like It, and *King Lear*, he
can fit them to the play. Sometimes, as there is
evidence, they were a sore trial to its integrity.
Costard is the conventional figure thinly disguised,
and he may quite rightly be played so. In his
very first scene, though he is Armado's man
brought by the constable for correction, he takes
all the jester's liberties with the King.

> *King.* Peace!
> *Costard.* Be to me and every man that dares not fight.
> *King.* No words!
> *Costard.* Of other men's secrets, I beseech you.

His attitude towards the Princess is the same.
The actor, then, is given a character to assume for

[1] And this need imply nothing rustic about him. He is
Armado's body-servant merely.

the play's consistency's sake; he must keep within it about as much as a low comedian did in Victorian farce or in Edwardian musical comedy. But no more. The play does not need another slow-spoken countryman. For that we have Dull, sparse of words and heavy of gait. Costard's is a nimble wit; we must feel that for diversion he makes himself out to be more of a fool than he is. And the actor himself must be skilful of speech and light of touch, as good jesters and stage-clowns were.

THE MUSIC

The indications of music and of the one dance are plain enough. Moth's ' Concolinel ' of Act III, Scene i, stands for a song, which no research has yet tracked. How anyone can doubt this it is hard to see. In the earlier scene Moth is asked to sing. There is no point whatever in his here disappointing Armado and the audience too with a comic catch-phrase. And why should Armado's comment upon it be

Sweet air !

Moreover, the stage-direction in the Folio definitely says "*A song.*" If what Shakespeare wrote or chose cannot be found, the producer must do the next best thing and make such a choice for himself as Shakespeare might have made. Many of the sources from which he picked ballads when he wanted them are open to us. A pity to have to do it, but obviously better than to leave a gap in the scene. The recurrent lightening of the play with lyrics sung or said is a part of its artistic economy.

The dance the blackamoors play, that Rosaline and the ladies will not respond to, may well be a 'French brawl.' A pity we miss the canarying with the feet; but the music probably lasts, as we have noted—the players in the background—till the finish of Boyet's apostrophe to the ladies' jigging tongues.

For the end we have song and dance both. "*Enter all*," say Quarto and Folio too. The play finishes, as a play of merry-making should, with everyone ranged for our last look at them. The simplest sort of a thing will serve best. Pedantry, cleverness, set poses, nice speaking, are all dropped. Armado, the incorrigible, the votary still, will have it, of course, that we are to hear a dialogue by the two learned men. The two learned men are to be found but a moment later dancing a hay with the best. Moth may sing the Spring song and Jaquenetta Winter's. Dull, it turns out, can do marvels on the pipe and tabor. Costard too, no doubt.

In fact, as there is no curtain to descend, no other-world of illusion to hide, the actors are already putting off the characters so lightly worn, and telling us that, after all, it is only a play. No, Armado does not dance. It is as if, the revels over, he stalked forward to speak an epilogue :

The words of Mercury are harsh after the songs of Apollo . . ¹

and could get no further. Are they ready to mock him again ? Then he bows to the quality :

You, that way; we, this way;

shepherds his motley flock and stalks after them.

JULIUS CÆSAR

JULIUS CÆSAR is the gateway through which Shakespeare passed to the writing of his five great tragedies. He had *Henry V* close behind him, *Hamlet* was not far ahead; between times he writes the three mature comedies, *Much Ado About Nothing*, *As You Like It* and *Twelfth Night*. In the themes, emphasis and methods of the work of this year or two we may watch the consummating development of his art.

Henry V gives the last touch to a hero of happy destiny. We might call it the latest play in which rhetoric for rhetoric's sake prevails. Shakespeare makes it occasion for a complaint of the inadequacy of his theatre to his theme. And it is, as one says, altogether a man's play. Woman's interest rules the three comedies; they contain much prose and make no extraordinary demands upon staging or acting. *Julius Cæsar*, again, is the manliest of plays. For the first time, too, Shakespeare fully submits his imagination to the great idea of Rome; new horizons seem to open to him, and there is to be no return to the comparative parochialism of the Histories. Nor, with this far mightier theme to develop, do we have any hint of discontent with the means to his hand. No chorus bows apology for the bringing of the foremost man of all the world upon such an unworthy scaffold.[1]

---

[1] It may well be, however, that with *Henry V* Shakespeare had surmised a patriot audience's instinct to demand for their hero trappings that a legendary foreigner like Cæsar could do well enough without.

And for Philippi, not only must a few ragged foils
suffice, we are back to the simple convention by
which whole armies face each other across the
stage. His playwright's mind is clearly not
troubled by such things now. What chiefly occu-
pies it in the planning and writing of *Julius Cæsar?*
He is searching, I think we may answer, for a hero,
for a new sort of hero. The story offers him more
than one, and does not force him to a choice.
He chooses, in the event, but haltingly. Very
significantly, however.

From the beginning Shakespeare's dramatic
development has lain in the discovering and
proving of the strange truth that in the theatre,
where external show seems everything, the most
effective show is the heart of a man. No need to
suppose it was lack of resource in stage furnishings
drove him to the drama of inward struggle,
triumph and defeat. That choice was innermostly
made, and no playwright worth calling one but
will make it on demand, whatever the theatre he
writes for. Henry V is not weakened as a character by lack of a pawing charger, but neither would
he be more of a hero set astride one. In himself
he is by no means all rhetoric; witness the scene
with his father and the soliloquy before Agincourt.
But his career has the power and the glory for an
end; and the parade of this, at its best, only
cumbers your hero—at its worst may make him
ridiculous. Henry finishes a fine figure of a man;
but long enough before Shakespeare has done all
he can with him, and our retrospect is rather of
the youthful junketings with Falstaff. For his
next hero it is in quite another direction he turns.
The next true hero is Hamlet: and Hamlet, fore-

shadowed in Rosaline's Romeo, in Richard II, in Jacques, is imminent in Brutus. A hero, let us be clear, is the character of which a dramatist, not morally, but artistically, most approves. Macbeth is a hero. Shakespeare's sympathy with Brutus does not imply approval of the murder of Cæsar; it only means that he ultimately finds the spiritual problem of the virtuous murderer the most interesting thing in the story. Brutus best interprets the play's theme: Do evil that good may come, and see what does come!

He is more interested, as he always has been, in character than in plot. He pays, goodness knows, small respect to the plots of the three contemporary comedies; they live by character alone. This, however, is history again, and plot must count. But it is not the homespun of Holinshed, nor the crude stuff of the *Famous Victories*. Plutarch gives him, not only the story he must abide by, but characters already charged with life. His task now is less to elaborate or invent than to capture and transmit as much of such events and such men as his little London theatre will hold. It is a feat of stagecraft to show us so many significant facets of this more than personal tragedy, a finer one to share out the best of the play's action among three chief characters and yet hardly lessen the strength of any of them.

But Shakespeare will never be too sure that he understands these Romans. He does not instinctively know their minds, as he knew Henry's or Hotspur's or Falstaff's. He is even capable of transcribing a fine-sounding passage from Plutarch and making something very like nonsense of it. He never gets to grips with Cæsar himself; whether

from shrewd judgment that he could not manœuvre
such greatness in the space he had to spare, or, as
looks more likely, from a sort of superstitious
respect for it. In which case—well, idols, as we
know, are apt to be wooden. Casca, raw from
Plutarch, has mettle enough to ride off with a scene
or two. Decius Brutus, Ligarius, Lucilius are
lifted whole from his pages. And the story itself
and its power, once Shakespeare is in its grip, can
breed from him moment after moment of pure
drama. In what play till now do the very
messengers and servants partake as they do in
this? But Brutus, Cassius and Antony, though
he has found them alive, he must set out to recreate
in his own terms. He does it by trial and error,
with a slip here and there, not disdaining a ready-
made patch that comes handy; the transformation
is never, perhaps, complete. But he seems to be
giving them their fling, tempting them to discover
themselves, passionate himself to know the truth
of them, whatever it may be, and ready to face it.
From no other play, probably, does he learn so
much in the writing. Collaborating with Plutarch
he can be critic and creator too. He finds what
is to him a new world of men, which he tests for
dramatic worth by setting it on this stage of his.
Julius Cæsar is an occasion to which, on the whole,
he rises; it is his greatest so far; it is a point of
advance, from which he never falls back.

THE CHARACTERS

Brutus

That the development of Brutus should be slow
is proper enough; such characters do not too

readily reveal themselves. Shakespeare builds the man up for us trait by trait; economically, each stroke of value, seldom an effect made merely for its own sake. With his usual care that the first things we learn shall be essential things, that very first sentence—measured, dispassionate, tinged with disdain—by which Brutus transmits to Cæsar the cry in the crowd:

> A soothsayer bids you beware the Ides of March,

gives us so much of the man to perfection; and its ominous weight is doubled in his mouth, its effect trebled by the innocent irony. Brutus draws aside from the procession to the games, withdrawn into himself.

> I am not gamesome: I do lack some part
> Of that quick spirit that is in Antony.
> Let me not hinder, Cassius, your desires;
> I'll leave you.

The strain of self-consciousness, that flaw in moral strength! A suspicion of pose! But self-consciousness can be self-knowledge; Shakespeare holds the scales even.

> Into what dangers would you lead me, Cassius,
> That you would have me seek into myself
> For that which is not in me?

Wisdom itself could give no apter warning. But is this next, in Brutus, something of a flourish, or in Shakespeare a touch of an earlier quality?

> What is it that you would impart to me?
> If it be aught toward the general good,
> Set honour in one eye and death i' the other,
> And I will look on both indifferently;
> For let the gods so speed me as I love
> The name of honour more than I fear death.

55

It will be captious to call it so. The lines come
hard upon the first of those shouts which are
perhaps the acclaiming of Cæsar as king. Brutus
is not a passionless man, though he may both
despise passion and dread it. A minute later he
is saying:

> I would not, so with love I might entreat you,
> Be any further mov'd.

Let the actor be wary, however, with that moment
of rhetoric; and let him see that he does not com-
pete with Cassius. For the jealous, passionate
Cassius, to whom and to whose mood eloquence
and rhetoric are natural, must inevitably dominate
this scene. Brutus, if we are to learn more of him,
needs a different setting. It is soon found. We
see him in the calm of night. He is kindly to his
sleepy page, gracious to his guests. We see him
alone with his wife, left all alone in the quiet with
his thoughts.

Much comment has been spent upon the first
soliloquy in this scene:

> It must be by his death: and, for my part,
> I know no personal cause to spurn at him . . .

Wise editors have found this inconsistent, some with
their own ideal of Brutus, some, rather more
reasonably, with the fully drawn figure of Shakespeare's play. But, at this stage of its development, why should we be puzzled? If the argument is super-subtle and unconvincing, why should
it not be? It may be that Shakespeare himself is
still fumbling to discover how this right-minded
man can commit his conscience to murder, but
why should his Brutus not be fumbling too?

This is how it will seem to an audience, surely; and editors' cleverness must not too far outstrip theirs.

The scene's marrow is the working of Brutus' mind, alone, in company. He is working it to some purpose now. But because it is, by disposition, a solitary mind, unused to interplay, and because the thoughts are not yet fused with emotion, that commoner currency between man and man, the scene moves a little stiffly and Brutus himself is stiff. Is not all this, again, dramatically right? Would he not speak his thoughts starkly, while the rest only listen and acquiesce?—though Cassius interposes one broken sentence of protest. They respect him, this upright, calm, self-contained man. He can command, but he cannot stir them; he is not a born leader. If the scene lacks suppleness and ease, one thought not prompting another revealingly, if it burns bright and hard, with never a flash into flame, so it would have been. But see how Shakespeare finally turns this very stiffness and suppression to a greater emotional account, when, after the silence Brutus keeps in the scene with Portia, the cry is wrung from him at last:

> You are my true and honourable wife,
> As dear to me as are the ruddy drops
> That visit my sad heart.

For let no one imagine that the overwhelming effect of this lies in the lines themselves. It has been won by his long impassiveness; by his listening, as we listen to Portia, till he and we too are overwrought. It is won by the courage with which Shakespeare holds his dramatic course.

Our sympathy with Brutus has next to weather the murder, through the planning and doing of which he stalks so nobly and disinterestedly and with such admirable self-control, and our interest in him to survive the emotional storm raised and ridden by Antony. This last might, one would think, sweep him for ever from his place in the play. The contriving of his recovery is, indeed, a most remarkable technical achievement. It depends upon several things. For one, upon Shakespeare's honest but ruthless treatment of Antony and his appeal to the mob; we too may be carried away by his eloquence, but the worth of it and of the emotions it rouses is kept clear to us all the time. For another : had he, as playwright, not been faithful to Brutus and his stern consistency, Brutus would fail him now; but now, the emotional debauch over, and all emotion cheapened, the stoic's chance is due. And the fourth act opens, it will be remembered, with a most unpleasant glimpse of Antony, the plain blunt man, triumphant. With that the stage is reset for Brutus and his tragedy.

In the clash with Cassius, Shakespeare, intent upon the truth of the man, shows him, we may protest, no undue favour.

Cassius. Most noble brother, you have done me wrong.
Brutus. Judge me, you gods! wrong I mine enemies?
And, if not so, how should I wrong a brother?
Cassius. Brutus, this sober form of yours hides wrongs;
And when you do them——
Brutus.   Cassius, be content;
Speak your griefs softly . . .

By the stoic's moral code it is Cassius himself, of course, who is in the wrong. But which of us might not side with him against this comrade, who, with war declared, protests justice to his enemies; and, with things going desperately for his side, must needs stiffen his stiff conscience against some petty case of bribery? Is this a time for pride in one's principles? Cæsar is dead—what matter now why or how?—and the spoils must be scrambled for, and the devil will take the hindmost. Cassius is no opportunist; yet so weary and distracted is he, that it almost comes to this with him. And he is answered:

> What! shall one of us
> That struck the foremost man of all this world
> But for supporting robbers, shall we now
> Contaminate our fingers with base bribes
> And sell the mighty space of our large honours
> For so much trash as may be grasped thus?

Noble sentiments! But is it a time to depreciate and dispirit your best friends, to refuse their apologies for having lost patience with you, to refuse even to lose your own in return? Brutus tries many of us as high as he tries Cassius. While what is so quelling to the impulsive, imperfect human being as the cold realism of the idealist?

Cassius. When Cæsar liv'd, he durst not thus have mov'd me.
Brutus. Peace, peace! you durst not so have tempted him.
Cassius. I durst not?
Brutus. No.
Cassius. What? durst not tempt him?
Brutus.   For your life you durst not.

Supercilious, unforgiving, and in the right! And when anger does rise in him, it is such a cold, deadly anger that poor passionate Cassius only breaks himself against it. Yet there is a com-

59

pelling power in the man, in his integrity of mind,
his truth to himself, in his perfect simplicity.
Even the detached, impersonal,

Cassius. You love me not.
Brutus. I do not like your faults.
Cassius. A friendly eye could never see such faults.
Brutus. A flatterer's would not . . .

though we may palate it no better than does
Cassius, is and sounds the simple truth. Cassius
cannot, somehow, be simple. The dagger and
the naked breast—who would be more surprised
than he, we feel, were he taken at his word?
But when Brutus relents his moral guard goes
down so utterly; there sweeps over him such a
sense of the pitifulness, not of Cassius and his
self-conscious passion only, but of all these petty
quarrels, of poor human nature itself, of his own
nature :

When I spoke that I was ill-tempered too.

It is a child making friends again with his fellow-
child.

Shakespeare has now all but prepared us for the
scene's great stroke; for the winning stroke in
Brutus' own cause with us. The quarrel is over
and the "jigging fool" has been dismissed.
Cassius took his turn as mentor when Brutus
snapped at the wretched poet.

Bear with him, Brutus, 'tis his fashion.

They set themselves to their business and call
for a bowl of wine ; we are in the vein of work-
aday. The one confesses to his " many griefs ";
the other responds with kindly platitude. And

60

to this comes the simple answer, three naked
words completing it:

Brutus. No man bears sorrow better: Portia is dead.
Cassius. Ha! Portia!
Brutus. She is dead.
Cassius. How 'scaped I killing when I crossed you so!

The seal is set upon Brutus' pre-eminence in the
play, which from now to its end is to be, in its
main current, the story of the doom towards
which he marches unregretful and clear-eyed.

Hamlet, we have said, originating in Richard
and Romeo, is imminent in Brutus; but the line
of descent is broken. Shakespeare, we may add,
fails in Brutus just where he will succeed in
Hamlet; he is instinctively searching, perhaps, to
express something which the poet in Hamlet will
accommodate, which the philosopher in Brutus
will not. Having lifted his heroic Roman to
this height, he leaves him, we must own, to stand
rather stockishly upon it. There is more than
one difficulty in the matter; and they were
bound to come to a head. Brutus reasons his way
through life, and prides himself upon suppressing
his emotions. But the Elizabethan conventions
of drama—and most others—are better suited to
the interpreting of emotion than thought. The
soliloquy, certainly, can be made a vehicle for
any sort of intimate disclosure. Shakespeare has
converted it already from a length of sheer rhetoric,
but not to turn it to a length of mere reasoning.
He could, indeed, better hold his audiences by fine
sounds than by mental process alone. For evidence
that he knows this well enough compare Brutus'
speech to the mob with Antony's in this very play.

61

Brutus' soliloquies in Act II are all but pure
thought, and in their place in the play, and at this
stage of his development, are well enough, are very
well. But—does Shakespeare feel?—you cannot
conduct a tragedy to its climax so frigidly. Had
Brutus been the play's true and sole hero a way
might have been found (by circling him, for
instance, with episodes of passion) to sustain the
emotional tension in very opposition to his stoic
calm. The murder of Cæsar and its sequel does
sweep the play up to a passionate height.
And the quarrel with the passionate Cassius, and
the fine device of the withheld news of Portia's
death, lift Brutus to a most heroic height, nor
with any betrayal of the consistent nature of the
man. But now we are at a standstill. Now, when
we expect, not—Heaven knows!—more argument,
but, Nemesis approaching, some deeper revelation,
some glimpse of the hero's very soul, this hero
stays inarticulate, or, worse, turns oracular. The
picturing of him is kept, now and to the end,
at a high pitch of simple beauty; but when the
final and intimate tragic issue should open out,
somehow it will not open. When Cæsar's ghost
appears:

Brutus. Speak to me what thou art.
Cæsar's Ghost. Thy evil spirit, Brutus.
Brutus.   Why com'st thou?
Cæsar's Ghost. To tell thee thou shalt see me at Philippi.
Brutus. Well: then I shall see thee again.
Cæsar's Ghost. Ay, at Philippi.
Brutus. Why, I will see thee at Philippi, then.

And before Philippi, a step nearer to the end of
this work the Ides of March began, we have from
the philosopher so confused a reflection on his fate

that we may well wonder whether Shakespeare himself, transcribing it from a mistranslated Plutarch, is quite certain what it means.[1]

We are left with

> O! that a man might know
> The end of this day's business ere it come;
> But it sufficeth that the day will end,
> And then the end is known.

That is the voice, they are all but the very words of Hamlet. He is to run the gamut of the mood of helpless doubt—the mood which has kept Hamlet our close kin through three disintegrating centuries —to more if not to better purpose. With Brutus it but masks the avoiding of a spiritual issue of which we know him to be well aware. And Shakespeare sends him to his death, a figure of gracious dignity, the noblest Roman of them all, but with eyes averted from the issue still.

> Countrymen,
> My heart doth joy that yet in all my life
> I found no man but he was true to me. . . .
> Night hangs upon mine eyes; my bones would rest,
> That have but labour'd to attain this hour.

The plain fact is, one fears, that Shakespeare, even if he can say he understands Brutus, can in this last analysis make nothing of him; and no phrase better fits a playwright's particular sort of failure. He has let him go his own reasoning way, has faithfully abetted him in it, has hoped that from beneath this crust of thought the fires will finally blaze. He can conjure up a flare or two, and the love and grief for Portia might promise a fusing of the man's whole nature in a tragic passion

[1] Furness collects four full pages of notes endeavouring to discover.

63

outpassing anything yet. But the essential tragedy centred in Brutus' own soul, the tragedy of the man who, not from hate, envy nor weakness, but

> . . . only, in a general honest thought
> And common good to all . . .

made one with the conspirators and murdered his friend; this, which Shakespeare rightly saw as the supremely interesting issue, comes to no more revelation than is in the weary

> . . . Cæsar, now be still:
> I killed not thee with half so good a will.

Shakespeare's own artistic disposition is not sufficiently attuned to this tragedy of intellectual integrity, of principles too firmly held. He can apprehend the nature of the man, but not, in the end, assimilate it imaginatively to his own. He is searching for the hero in whom thought and emotion will combine and contend on more equal terms; and when the end of Brutus baffles him, here is Hamlet, as we have seen, all waiting to begin. For the rest, he at least reaps the reward, a better than Brutus did, of integrity and consistency. He never falsifies the character, and, in its limited achievement, it endures and sustains the play to the end. He had preserved, we may say, for use at need, his actor's gift of making effective things he did not fully understand; and the Brutus of the play will make call enough on the actor even should he know a little more about Brutus the Stoic than Shakespeare did.

Cassius

Cassius is blest—and cursed—with a temperament. He is compounded, that is to say, of qualities contradictory enough to keep him in a ferment. He is passionate, but self-conscious; he is an egoist and yet clear-sighted, and yet unwise. Does he really admire Brutus? He plays on his weaknesses and follows his lead. He is self-willed, but he feeds on sympathy. He is brave and as nervous as a cat. He sways between more obvious inconsistencies besides. For all his cleverness he is simple; and rash simplicity is his doom at last. He kills Cæsar remorselessly; but he swears—and it is no boast—that he would take his own life as soon rather than suffer shame. He would take Antony's too, from pure policy; yet in the flush and confusion of a bloody triumph he can pause to think of the danger innocent old Publius may run. He tricks Brutus, his friend, by the letters laid in the Prætor's chair and thrown in at the window; but when the rest go smiling to lure Cæsar to death, though he sees to it they go, he holds back.[1] Truly it might rather be from caution than conscience, for he is not apt at hiding his feelings; and he knows he has not hidden them from Cæsar, whose sharp eye caught his acrid looks as he passed him coming from the games; while Cassius, as sharp, guessed that the low talk with Antony was of him. But though he knows that Cæsar " bears him hard " he talks the most reckless treason to Casca. It is well-calculated recklessness, however. He has gauged that seeming tardiness aright; he strikes fire from the flint. In all he is alert and vibrant; he can do anything but do nothing.

[1] His absence, of course, is in question. It may be that the stage direction of the Folio is faulty. But, if he is there, it is unlikely that Cæsar, naming the others, would ignore him, or that he, being ignored, would stay silent.

What better sort of character, then, for getting
such a play as this under way? But later, if it is
not to be let peter out, or if the whole play is not
to be given up to its displaying, it will need careful
manœuvring. For nothing is so monotonous as
excitement, and brilliance unceasing is as painful
as the glare of the sun on the sea. The first histrionic flaw in Cassius shows when, after this vivid
opening, as valuable to the character as the play,
Shakespeare, at a critical juncture, writes fifteen
mechanical lines. It is no more than this; but
with them the dramatic life of the man fades, and
will be the harder, its earlier moments remembered, to revive. Compare the soliloquy:

Well, Brutus, thou art noble . . .

with anything in the scene which it ends. It is a
fair enough statement, no doubt, of what Cassius
is thinking and, for a moment, feeling. But in
dramatic value it falls to the level of one of those
plot-forwarding discourses, crude conveniences of
Elizabethan stagecraft, that Shakespeare had long
known how to turn to finer account. Cassius is
naturally forthcoming in company; nervous,
passionate, self-conscious, it stimulates him to
expression. Left alone, did he fall suddenly
inarticulate, or stand resistant to his author's
immediate use for him? Was Shakespeare then too
impatient to stay for the discovery of another
Cassius, the man intimately himself, to remould
the crucible of character in which these things
the plot needed making plain could be fused?
It would seem so. And this chance of intimacy
missed—for which, with so much of Cassius
revealed, we were all alert—though we learn

more about him soon, we do not somehow come to know him better. In the scenes that follow we learn of his recklessness (in unbosoming himself to Casca), his impatient arrogance (in his treatment of Cinna), his quick despair (when Popilius Lena whispers to Cæsar), his shrewd prevision (of the danger in Antony the orator, in an Antony left alive and unbought). The iteration, the monotony of temper and attitude can be dramatically justified; Cassius is obsessed by the one idea, and he is the goad by which the play's action is driven ahead. Nevertheless, that chance missed to show us the pulsing heart of the man, the actor will need to play with skill and discretion if this next stretch of the part, from the soliloquy to the third act, is not to be a little tiresome. The opening scene has been irresistibly effective. It will be wise now, by a certain general restraint, by an emphasis of each new trait just sufficient to keep the figure an harmonious whole, to seem to promise more intimate things to come. They do come, when Shakespeare takes fresh breath for the fourth act ; we then have another plenary picture of Cassius in word and action, a companion study, if a reverse of the medal. And such men as he are doubtless better to be interpreted by setting them in sharply contrasted situations; for they do not develop, and the truest thing about them is that, though their circumstances change, they do not. It is the strength and the weakness of Cassius that he can strip his mind bare to men; but perhaps, after all, there was nothing innermost for that soliloquy to disclose ? Compare the two scenes between the two comrades. The tragedy of the man is that he has not changed,

6   67

though things have changed with him. He was
jealous of Cæsar then; he is jealous of Brutus
now, of his friend as of his enemy. Cæsar was
right about him, it seems.

> Such men as he be never at heart's ease
> Whiles they behold a greater than themselves. . . .

He slights Brutus' generalship as he mocked at
Cæsar's courage. He is as quick, as shrewd, as
shrewish as ever. But while once it was:

> Well, honour is the subject of my story,

now he is politicly pleading for a rogue; even his
own honesty is in question. And the old eloquent
candour turns, in spite of him, to blustering, to
scolding, to crude inarticulate assertion. Yet even
while he rages he knows he is in the wrong. He
has had his way, but he is a beaten man, whether
Philippi be won or no, and the battle-field has
been within him. The brilliant Cassius, put
to the test, lacks character, that inexplicable
virtue. He knows this too; his pride is a mask.
At the first touch of compassion—it is very lovable!
—he surrenders like a child.

Cassius.   O Brutus !
Brutus.   What's the matter?
Cassius.   Have you not love enough to bear with me
            When that rash humour which my mother gave me
            Makes me forgetful?

So from now on—and not now from mere policy
—he will follow magnanimity's mistaken lead, even
though he knows it to be mistaken. The tragedy
of unbalanced brilliance! He is a humbled man
at heart now; a man weary of himself, the pride,

the tortuous cleverness purged out of him; and
in their stead, a craving for affection.

Cassius.   O my dear brother,
    This was an ill beginning of the night:
    Never come such division 'tween our souls!
    Let it not, Brutus.
Brutus.   Everything is well.
Cassius. Good-night, my lord.
Brutus.   Good-night, good brother.

The " elder soldier " abases himself before the
younger, though Brutus, with that kind " good
brother," would prevent him; the cynical Cassius
has turned remorseful child.

Thus it is with these catastrophic natures. They
spend themselves freely, while they demand much
of the world; they plague their friends—who are
found next moment defending them—and are
tolerable neither in success nor defeat. Why, we
ask exasperatedly, should anyone put up with
them? This scene of the quarrel is Shakespeare's
answer; a playwright's, not a moralist's answer.
Let Cassius be never so intolerable, we no more
cease to care for him than Brutus does. His faults
are too human; they make us—most of us—kin to
him, and kind.

Let us note further that, for an end, Shakespeare
works no mechanical conversion of wolf to lamb.
" Old Cassius still," mocks Antony, when the two
meet again. The nervous relief of a good quarrel
with Brutus does indeed seem to give both virtues
and asperities a new lease of life.

    For I am fresh of spirit and resolved
    To meet all perils very constantly

—though voice and look may be weary still. Then
the battle is joined; and he kills his own standard-

bearer in the fury of defeat, and himself in the impatience of his despair. Old Cassius still!

Antony

There is a tide in the affairs of men,
Which, taken at the flood, leads on to fortune. . . .

Mark Antony cannot always talk so wisely, but he takes the tide that Brutus loses. He is a born opportunist, and we see him best in the light of his great opportunity. He stands contrasted with both Cassius and Brutus, with the man whom his fellows respect the more for his aloofness, and with such a rasping colleague as Cassius must be. Antony is, above all things, a good sort.

Shakespeare keeps him in ambush throughout the first part of the play. Up to the time when he faces the triumphant conspirators he speaks just thirty-three words. But there have already been no less than seven separate references to him, all significant. And this careful preparation culminates as significantly in the pregnant message he sends by his servant from the house to which it seems he has fled, bewildered by the catastrophe of Cæsar's death. Yet, as we listen, it is not the message of a very bewildered man. Antony, so far, is certainly—in what we might fancy would be his own lingo—a dark horse. And, though we may father him on Plutarch, to English eyes there can be no more typically English figure than the sportsman turned statesman, but a sportsman still. Such men range up and down our history. Antony is something besides, however, that we used to flatter ourselves was not quite so English. He can be, when occasion serves, the perfect demagogue. Nor has Shakespeare any illusions as to what the harsher needs of politics may convert your sportsman once he is out to kill. The conspirators are fair game doubtless. But Lepidus, a little later, will be the carted stag.

> A barren-spirited fellow; one that feeds
> On abject orts and imitations,
> Which, out of use and staled by other men,
> Begin his fashion: do not talk of him
> But as a property . . .

to serve the jovial Antony's turn! This is your good sort, your sportsman, your popular orator, stripped very bare.

The servant's entrance with Antony's message, checking the conspirators' triumph, significant in its insignificance, is the turning-point of the play.[1] But Shakespeare plucks further advantage from it. It allows him to bring Antony out of ambush completely effective and in double guise; the message foreshadows him as politician, a minute later we see him grieving deeply for his friend's death. There is, of course, nothing incompatible in the two aspects of the man, but the double impression is all-important. He must impress us as uncalculatingly abandoned to his feelings, risking his very life to vent them. For a part of his strength lies in impulse; he can abandon himself to his feelings, as Brutus the philosopher cannot. Moreover, this bold simplicity is his safe-conduct now. Were the conspirators not impressed by it, did it not obliterate for the moment his politic side, they might well and wisely take him at his word and get rid of him. And at the back of his mind Antony has this registered clearly enough. It must be with

[1] As Moulton demonstrates in an admirable passage.

something of the sportsman's—and the artist's—
reckless joy that he flings the temptation at them.

> Live a thousand years
> I shall not find myself so apt to die;
> No place will please me so, no mean of death,
> As here by Cæsar, and by you cut off,
> The choice and master spirits of this age.

He means it; but he knows, as he says it, that there
is no better way of turning the sword of a choice
and master spirit aside. It is this politic, shadowed
aspect of Antony that is to be their undoing; so
Shakespeare was concerned to keep it clear at the
back of our minds. Therefore he impressed it on
us first by the servant's speech, leaving Antony
himself free to win us and the conspirators both.

Not that the politician does not begin to peep
pretty soon. He tactfully ignores the cynicism of
Cassius,

> Your voice shall be as strong as any man's
> In the disposing of new dignities.

But by Brutus' reiterated protest that Cæsar was
killed in pure kindness what realist, what ironist
—and Antony is both—would not be tempted?

> I doubt not of your wisdom.
> Let each man render me his bloody hand.

And, in bitter irony, he caps their ritual with his
own. It is the ritual of friendship, but of such a
friendship as the blood of Cæsar, murdered by his
friends, may best cement. To Brutus the place of
honour in the compact; to each red-handed
devotee his due; and last, but by no means least,
in Antony's love shall be Trebonius who drew him

away while the deed was done. And so to the final, most fitting apostrophe:

Gentlemen all!

Emotion subsided, the politician plays a good game. They shall never be able to say he approved their deed; but he is waiting, please, for those convincing reasons that Cæsar was dangerous. He even lets slip a friendly warning to Cassius that the prospect is not quite clear. Then, with yet more disarming frankness, comes the challenging request to Brutus to let him speak in the market-place. As he makes it, a well-calculated request! For how can Brutus refuse, how admit a doubt that the Roman people will not approve this hard service done them? Still, that there may be no doubt at all, Brutus will first explain everything to his fellow-citizens himself, lucidly and calmly. When reason has made sure of her sway, the emotional, the ' game-some ' Antony may do homage to his friend.

Be it so;
I do desire no more,

responds Antony, all docility and humility, all gravity—though if ever a smile could sharpen words, it could give a grim edge to these. So they leave him with dead Cæsar.

In this contest thus opened between the man of high argument and the instinctive politician, between principle (mistaken or not) and opportunism, we must remember that Antony can be by no means confident of success. He foresees chaos. He knows, if these bemused patriots do not, that it takes more than correct republican doctrines to replace a great man. As to this

73

Roman mob—this citizenry, save the mark!—whoever knows which way it will turn? The odds are
on the whole against him. But he'll try his luck;
Octavius, though, had better keep safely out of
the way meanwhile. All his senses are sharpened
by emergency. Before ever Octavius' servant can
speak he has recognised the fellow and guessed the
errand. Shakespeare shows us his mind at its
swift work, its purposes shaping.

> Passion, I see, is catching; for mine eyes,
> Seeing those beads of sorrow stand in thine,
> Began to water

—which is as much as to say that if the sight of
Cæsar's body can so move the man and the man's
tears so move him, who knows to what his own
passion may not move the people in the market-
place presently! His imagination, once it takes
fire, flashes its way along, not by reason's slow
process though in reason's terms.[1]

[1] How many modern actors upon their picture stage, with
its curtain to close a scene for them pat upon some triumphant top note, have brought this one to its end upon the
familiar, tremendous, breathless apostrophe (did Shakespeare ever pen such another sentence?) that begins,

> Woe to the hand that shed this costly blood;
> Over thy wounds now do I prophesy . . .

But to how untimely an end! The tradition of Shakespeare's
theatre forbade such effects and in this instance its mechanism
also. Cæsar's body is lying on the main stage, and must be
removed, and it will take at least two people to carry it.
Here is one sufficient reason for the arrival of Octavius'
servant. But as ever with Shakespeare, and with any artist
worth his salt, limitation is turned to advantage. If dead
Cæsar is to be the mainspring of the play's further action,
what more forceful way could be found of making this
plain than, for a finish to the scene, to state the new theme
of Octavius' coming, Cæsar's kin and successor?

To what he does move the people we know:
and it will be worth while later to analyse the
famous speech, that triumph of histrionics. For
though the actor of Antony must move us with it
also—and he can scarcely fail to—Shakespeare has
set him the further, harder, and far more important
task of showing us an Antony the mob never see,
of making him clear to us, moreover, even while
we are stirred by his eloquence, of making crystal
clear to us by what it is we are stirred. It would,
after all, be pretty poor playwriting and acting
which could achieve no more than a plain piece
of mob oratory, however gorgeous; a pretty poor
compliment to an audience to ask of it no
subtler response than the mob's. But to show
us, and never for a moment to let slip from our
sight, the complete and complex Antony, impulsive and calculating, warm-hearted and callous,
aristocrat, sportsman and demagogue, that will
be for the actor an achievement indeed; and
the playwright has given him all the material
for it.

Shakespeare himself knows, no one better, what
mere histrionics may amount to. He has been
accused of a too great contempt for the mob; he
might then have felt something deeper than contempt for the man who could move the mob by
such means; he may even have thought Brutus
made the better speech. Antony, to be sure, is
more than an actor; for one thing he writes his
own part as he goes along. But he gathers the
ideas for it as he goes too, with no greater care
for their worth than the actor need have so long as
they are effective at the moment. He lives abundantly in the present, his response to its call is

unerring. He risks the future. How does the
great oration end?

> Mischief, thou art afoot;
> Take thou what course thou wilt.

A wicked child, one would say, that has whipped
up his fellow-children to a riot of folly and violence.
That is one side of him. But the moment after
he is off, brisk, cool and business-like, to play
the next move in the game with that very cool
customer, Octavius.

He has had no tiresome principles to consult
or to expound.

> I only speak right on. . . .

he boasts;

> . . . I tell you that which you yourselves do know.

An admirable maxim for popular orators and
popular writers too! There is nothing aloof,
nothing superior about Antony. He may show
a savage contempt for this man or that; he has
a sort of liking for men in the mass. He is, in
fact, the common man made perfect in his common-
ness; but perceptive of himself as of his fellows,
and yet content.

What follows upon his eloquent mourning for
Cæsar? When the chaos in Rome has subsided he
ropes his " merry fortune " into harness. It is
not a very pleasant colloquy with which the fourth
act opens.

Antony. These many then shall die; their names are
     pricked.
Octavius. Your brother too must die; consent you,
     Lepidus?
Lepidus. I do consent.
Octavius.   Prick him down, Antony.

Lepidus. Upon condition Publius shall not live,
Who is your sister's son, Mark Antony.
Antony. He shall not live; look, with a spot I damn him.

The conspirators have, of course, little right
to complain. But four lines later we learn
that Lepidus himself, when his two friends have
had their use of him, is to fare not much better
than his brother—than the brother he has himself
just given so callously to death! Can he complain
either, then? This is the sort of beneficence the
benevolent Brutus has let loose on the world.

But Antony finishes the play in fine form;
victorious in battle, politicly magnanimous to a
prisoner or two, and ready with a resounding
tribute to Brutus, now that he lies dead. Not in
quite such fine form, though; for the shadow of
that most unsportsmanlike young man Octavius
is already moving visibly to his eclipse.

These, then, are the three men among whom
Shakespeare divides this dramatic realm; the
idealist, the egoist, the opportunist. The contrast
between them must be kept clear in the acting by
all that the actors do and are, for upon its tension
the living structure of the play depends. And, it
goes without saying, they must be shown to us as
fellow-creatures, not as abstractions from a dead
past. For so Shakespeare saw them; and, if he
missed something of the mind of the Roman, yet
these three stand with sufficient truth for the sum
of the human forces, which in any age, and in ours
as in his, hold the world in dispute.

Octavius Cæsar

He tags to the three another figure; and perhaps nothing in the play is better done within its

limits, than is the outline of Octavius Cæsar, the
man who in patience will reap when all this bitter
seed has been sown. He appears three times,
speaks some thirty lines, and not one of them is
wasted. We see him first with Antony and
Lepidus. He watches them trade away the lives
of their friends and kinsmen. And when Antony,
left alone with him, proposes to 'double-cross'
Lepidus, he only answers,

> You may do your will;
> But he's a tried and valiant soldier.

It is the opening of a window into this young man's
well-ordered mind. Lepidus is a good soldier,
he approves of Lepidus. But Antony is powerful
for the moment, it won't do to oppose Antony.
Lepidus must suffer then. Still, should things
turn out differently, let Antony remember that
this was his own proposal, and that Octavius never
approved of it.[1]

By the next scene, however, this quiet youth has
grown surer—not of himself, that could hardly be,
but of his place amid the shifting of events.

Antony. Octavius, lead your battle softly on,
Upon the left hand of the even field.
Octavius. Upon the right hand, I; keep thou the left.
Antony. Why do you cross me in this exigent?
Octavius. I do not cross you; but I will do so.

He is quite civil about it; but he means to have his
way, his chosen place in the battle and chief credit
for the victory. And Antony does not argue the

[1] *Julius Cæsar* begins the cycle of Shakespeare's greater
plays, and *Antony and Cleopatra* ends it. The later relations
of Octavius and Antony are implicit in this little scene. The
realist, losing grip, will find himself 'out-realised' by his
pupil.

point. When the opponents in the coming battle
are face to face, Cassius and Antony, and even
Brutus may outscold each the other for past
offences. The practical Octavius, with a mind
to the present and to his own future, is impatient
of such childishness.

> Come, come, the cause: if arguing make us sweat,
> The proof of it will turn to redder drops.
> Look, I draw sword against conspirators:
> When think you that the sword goes up again?
> Never, till Cæsar's three-and-thirty wounds
> Be well aveng'd; or till another Cæsar
> Have added slaughter to the sword of traitors.

This is the first time he has spoken out, and he
speaks to some purpose. Nor does he give place
to Antony again. When we see them together
for the last time in victorious procession, Octavius
has the lead.

> All that serv'd Brutus, I will entertain them.

' I,' not ' we.' And Shakespeare gives him the
play's last word.

Cæsar

What now of the great shadow of Cæsar which
looms over the whole? Let us admit that, even
while he lives and speaks, it is more shadow than
substance. Is it too harsh a comment that Cæsar
is in the play merely to be assassinated? But to
have done better by him would have meant,
would it not, doing worse by the play as it is
planned? Certainly to centre every effort—and
it could hardly be done with less—upon presenting
to us

> . . . the foremost man of all this world

79

and then to remove him at the beginning of Act III would leave a gap which no new interest could fill. But there are innate difficulties in the putting of any great historical figure upon the stage: and these, as it happens, would have pressed hard upon Shakespeare just at this time. He had left behind him the writing of that formal rhetoric which was the accepted dramatic full dress for the great man. He was moulding his verse to the expressing of emotion, fitting his whole method to the showing of intimate human conflict. Now a great man's greatness seldom exists in his personal relations. To depict it, then, the dramatist will be thrown back on description, or narrative, or on the effect of the greatness upon people around. The last expedient may shift our interest to the surrounding people themselves. Narrative in excess is tiresome. And as to description; the great man himself, in the person of his actor, is too apt to belie it. Keep him immobile and taciturn, and the play will halt. But if he talks of his own achievements he will seem a boaster. And if he is always seen in action we can have no picture of the inner man. The convention of Greek drama offers some escape from these dilemmas; for there the man is, so to speak, made in his greatness a symbol of himself, and in a symbol one may sum up a truth. Shakespeare had the refuge of soliloquy. Show us the heart of a Cæsar, though, by that means, and where will our interest in the self-revealings of a Brutus be? And it is, we have argued, upon Brutus' spiritual tragedy that Shakespeare's best thoughts are fixed. He comes, therefore, to showing us a Cæsar seen somewhat from Brutus' point of view; a noble figure and eloquent, but our knowledge of him stays skin-deep. It is historically possible, of course, that the virtue had gone out of Cæsar, that no more was left now than this façade of a great man. But we need not credit Shakespeare with the theory. Quite certainly he wishes to show us the accepted Cæsar of history. The innate difficulty of doing so may defeat him; the limitations of the play, as he has planned it, must. And if he has to choose, and it becomes a question of his play's safety, Cæsar will count no more with him than any other character.

But it follows that, as he cannot attempt to do Cæsar dramatic justice, the more we see of him the worse it is. For the devices by which his supremacy can be made effective are soon exhausted and do not bear repetition. The start is excellent. What could be more impressive than that first procession across the stage? Here Shakespeare tries the taciturn-immobile method, and couples it with a strict simplicity of speech; all one can call a trick is the repetition of the name, and Cæsar's own use of it, and even this is legitimate enough. While, for a finish, the confronting of the Sooth-sayer:

Cassius. Fellow, come from the throng; look upon
        Cæsar.
Cæsar. What say'st thou to me now? Speak once again.
Soothsayer. Beware the Ides of March.
Cæsar. He is a dreamer, let us leave him: pass.

What could be better? The last line is pure gold.

The episode of the returning procession is as good. That sidelong perceptive survey of Cassius with its deep-biting humour:

Let me have men about me that are fat,
Sleek-headed men, and such as sleep a-nights.
Yond Cassius has a lean and hungry look;
He thinks too much: such men are dangerous . . .

The yet deeper-bitten realism of

He reads much;
He is a great observer, and he looks
Quite through the deeds of men; he loves no plays,
As thou dost, Antony; he hears no music;
Seldom he smiles, and smiles in such a sort
As if he mock'd himself, and scorn'd his spirit
That could be mov'd to smile at any thing.
Such men as he be never at heart's ease
Whiles they behold a greater than themselves,
And therefore are they very dangerous.

The precise simplicity of thought and language
mark the man raised above his fellows. Do we
need, then,

I rather tell thee what is to be fear'd
Than what I fear, for always I am Cæsar.

But it is from this very moment that the direct-
picturing of Cæsar turns to talk about Cæsar by
Cæsar. Fine talk; but the living man is lost in
it. For a line or two he may emerge, only to be
lost again in some such operatic sonority as

Cæsar should be a beast without a heart
If he should stay at home to-day for fear.
No, Cæsar shall not; danger knows full well
That Cæsar is more dangerous than he:
We are two lions littered in one day,
And I the elder and more terrible;
And Cæsar shall go forth

—while the Olympian speech in the Senate-house
leaves one a little surprised that a moment later
blood can be supposed to flow from him. Shakespeare, in fact, has now slipped not merely into this
82

queer *oratio obliqua* but back to the discarded rhetoric
for its own sake, though the writing of the characters round Cæsar stays directly dramatic enough.
The actor must effect what sort of reconciliation
he can between Shakespeare's intention and
accomplishment, between this simulacrum of
greatness and the dramatic life around. To
think of Cæsar as now no more than an empty shell,
reverberating hollowly, the life and virtue gone out
of him, is one way. It must weaken the play a
little; for will it be so desperate an enterprise to
conspire against such a Cæsar? Or is such a frigid
tyranny the more dangerous of the two? But the
subtlety of that interpretation is worse.

Casca and the rest

Among the men no other characters reach
primary importance. Casca is effective rather
than important, and the only question about
him is of the break from prose to verse (as between
Act I, Scenes ii and iii), which points a kindred but
hardly warrantable break in the composition of
the character itself. It is all very well to say with
Dowden that Casca appears in the storm with his
" superficial garb of cynicism dropt," and that,
while dramatic consistency may be a virtue,
Shakespeare here gives us an instance of " a piece
of higher art, the dramatic inconsistency of his
characters." If it were so the thing would still be
very clumsily done. What means is the actor given
of showing that this is a dramatic inconsistency?
We never see one flutter of that superficial
garb of cynicism again. Casca remains hereafter the commonplace Casca of the storm scene;
the humorous blunt fellow seems forgotten quite.

7   83

Certainly we have had Cassius' apology for him,
that he

. . . puts on this tardy form . . .

But the whole passage in which that occurs is
weak and mechanical, and it might arguably have
been written in to excuse the clumsiness of the
change. The actor must do what he can to weld
the two halves of the man together; but it is doubtful whether he can make this " piece of higher
art " very evident to an audience.

The producer must remember that nine-tenths
of the play is, so to speak, orchestrated for men
only; the greater the need in the casting of the
parts to set them in due contrast with each other.
The sort of acting a part needs is usually made
plain enough; if not by some reference, acting itself
will test this. For instance, if nothing definitely
directs us to make the Flavius and Marullus of
the first scene a mild man and a masterfully noisy
one, yet in the acting they will be found to answer
effectively to that difference. For the casting of
Cicero, on the other hand, we have definite, if
mainly *ex post facto* direction; his elderly dry
irony is set, when the two meet, in strong contrast
with the new ebullient Casca. It is to be noted, by
the way, that Shakespeare, history apart, thinks of
the conspirators as fairly young men. By theatrical
tradition Caius Ligarius is made old as well as ill,
but there is nothing to warrant this (for an ague
does not warrant it), nor any dramatic gain in it.

Cinna the poet is specified plainly enough in
the dandification of

What is my name? Whither am I going? Where do I
dwell? Am I a married man or a bachelor? Then, to
answer every man directly and briefly, wisely and truly;
wisely I say I am a bachelor.

84

The nameless poet of Act IV must be even more eccentric if his flying visit is to be made effective. Cassius calls him a cynic. He is, one supposes, a shabby ballad-mongering fellow; his modern instance shuffles through the *cafés* of Montmartre to-day. Shakespeare, rapt in this world of great doings, is a little hard on poets—as some poets are apt to be.

The soldiers that belong to the play's last phase, Messala, Lucilius, Titinius, young Cato, Pindarus, Volumnius, Strato and the rest, can all be known for what they are by considering what they do. In no play, I think, does Shakespeare provide, in such a necessarily small space, for such a vivid array. As parts of a battle-piece, the unity of the subject harmonises them, but within that harmony each is very definitely and effectively himself.

Calpurnia and Portia

The boy Lucius has sometimes been played by a woman. This is an abomination. Let us not forget, on the other hand, that Calpurnia was written to be played by a boy. Producers are inclined to make a fine figure of her, to give her (there being but two women in the play) weight and importance, to fix on some well-proportioned lady, who will wear the purple with an air. But Shakespeare's intention is as plain as daylight; and in a part of twenty-six lines there can be no compromise, it must be hit or miss. Calpurnia is a nervous, fear-haunted creature. Nor does she, like Portia, make any attempt to conceal her fears. She is desperate and helpless. Portia, with her watchful constancy, can win Brutus' secret from him. Cæsar treats Calpurnia like a child. Her

JULIUS CÆSAR

pleading with him is a frightened child's pleading;
her silence when Decius and the rest come to fetch
him to the Senate-house—silence broken, for better
emphasis, by just one cry—is as pathetic in its
helplessness. What happens to her during the
remainder of the scene? We have but one cue,
Cæsar's

> Give me my robe, for I will go.

This is the last line of a speech to Calpurnia, but
perhaps it is spoken to the servant who, a minute
or so before, brought the news from the augurers.
I would rather take it, though, as a hint for dividing her from the group of eager men who are
now surrounding her husband. She stands tremulous, watching him go in to taste some wine with
these good friends; then she goes herself to do his
bidding for the last time. Failing the right sort
of Calpurnia, quite half the dramatic value of
her scene will be lost.

A quiet beauty is the note of Portia, and Shakespeare sounds it at once. Her appearance is
admirably contrived. The conspirators have gone,
Brutus is alone again, and the night's deep stillness
is recalled.

> Boy! Lucius! Fast asleep? It is no matter;
> Enjoy the honey-heavy dew of slumber:
> Thou hast no figures nor no fantasies
> Which busy care draws in the brains of men;
> Therefore thou sleep'st so sound.

But so softly she comes, that for all the stillness
he is unaware of her, until the soft voice, barely
breaking it, says,

> Brutus, my lord!

Portia is a portrait in miniature. But how suited
the character itself is to such treatment, and how

86

Shakespeare subdues his power to its delicacy! The whole play is remarkable for simplicity and directness of speech; nothing could exemplify her better. For she is seen not as a clever woman, nor is she witty, and she speaks without coquetry of her " once-commended beauty." She is home-keeping and content; she is yielding, but from good sense, which she does not fear will seem weakness. Her friends perhaps call her a dull woman. But she has a dignity of soul and an innate courage that might well leave the cleverest of them humble.

Note how everything in the scene—not the words and their meaning only—contributes to build up this Portia. The quiet entrance, the collected thought and sustained rhythm of her unchecked speech, the homely talk of supper-time and of the impatient Brutus scratching his head and stamping, and of his present risk of catching cold; nothing more wonderful than this is the foundation for the appeal to

> . . . that great vow
> Which did incorporate and make us one . . .

Nor does the appeal at its very height disturb the even music of the verse. For with her such feelings do not ebb and flow; they lie deep down, they are a faith. She is, as we should say, all of a piece; and her very gentleness, her very reasonableness is her strength. Even her pride has its modesty.

> I grant I am a woman, but, withal,
> A woman that Lord Brutus took to wife;
> I grant I am a woman; but, withal,
> A woman well-reputed, Cato's daughter;
> Think you I am no stronger than my sex,
> Being so father'd and so husbanded?

The repeated phrase and the stressed consonants give the verse a sudden vigour; they contrast with the drop back to simplicity of

> Tell me your counsels, I will not disclose 'em.
> I have made strong proof of my constancy,
> Giving myself a voluntary wound
> Here, in the thigh: can I bear that with patience
> And not my husband's secrets?

To this, with imperceptibly accumulating force, with that one flash of pride for warning, the whole scene has led. A single stroke, powerful in its reticence, as fine in itself as it is true to Portia.

Then, lest she should seem too good to be true, Shakespeare adds a scene of anti-climax; of a Portia confessing to weakness, all nerves, miserably conscious that her page's sharp young eyes are fixed on her; outfacing, though, the old soothsayer, and, with a final effort, spiritedly herself again. While, for one more touch of truth, he gives us,

> O Brutus!
> The heavens speed thee in thine enterprise.

Murder is the enterprise, and Cato's daughter knows it. But he is her Brutus, so may the heavens speed him even in this.

THE PLAY'S STRUCTURE

There is a powerful ease in the construction of *Julius Cæsar* which shows us a Shakespeare master of his means, and it is the play in which the boundaries of his art begin so markedly to widen. We find in it, therefore, a stagecraft, not of a too accustomed perfection, but bold and free. The theme calls forth all his resources and inspires their fresh and vigorous use; yet it does not strain them, as some later and, if greater, less accommodating themes are to do. We may here study Elizabethan stagecraft, as such, almost if not quite at its best; and a close analysis of the play's action, the effects in it and the way they are gained—a task for the producer in any case—will have this further interest.

Plutarch was a godsend to Shakespeare. Rome, Cæsar and high heroic verse, one knows what such a mixture may amount to in the theatre ; though we may suppose that, with his lively mind, he would never have touched the subject had he not found that admirable historian, who, with happy familiarity, tucks an arm in ours, so to speak, and leads us his observant, anecdotic way, humanising history, yet never diminishing its magnificence. Plutarch's genius, in fact, is closely allied to Shakespeare's own, with its power to make, by a touch or so of nature, great men and simple, present and past, the real and the mimic world, one kin. And this particular power was in the ascendant with Shakespeare now.

He redraws the outline of the story more simply, but he cannot resist crowding characters in. What wonder, when they are all so striking, and he knows he can make a living man out of a dozen lines of dialogue. The fifth act is a galaxy of such creations. We may own, on the other hand, that Artemidorus and the soothsayer are little more than living stage furniture, and that the poet of Act IV is a mere irruption into the play, a species of human ordnance shot off. But much of the play's virtue lies in the continual invention and abundant vitality of these details of character and action, upon which the rarer life, so to call it, of the chief characters is sustained. There is no formal mechanism of plot, the action moves forward with a varied rhythm, upon an ebb and flow of minor event that is most lifelike. The whole play is alive; it is alive in every line.

Elizabethan stagecraft, with its time freedom and space freedom, gives the playwright great scope for manœuvring minor character and incident. He may conjure a character into sudden prominence, and be done with it as suddenly. He has not, as in the modern ' realistic ' theatre, to relate it to the likelihoods of hard-and-fast time and place. The modern dramatist plans his play by large divisions, even as the Greek dramatist did. Time and place must suit the need of his chief characters; if minor ones can't be accommodating they can't be accommodated, that's all. The Elizabethan dramatist has his story to tell, and the fate of the chief figures in it to determine. But, as long as the march of the story is not stayed, he may do pretty well what he likes by the way. The modern dramatist thinks of his play constructively in acts; and the scenes must accommodate themselves to the act, as the acts to the play as a whole. The Elizabethan would instinctively do the contrary. This is not to say that a play did not commonly move to some larger rhythm than the incidental. Every playwright, every sort of artist indeed, feels for the form which will best accommodate his idea, and will come to prefer the comprehensive form. But whether this rhythm with Shakespeare resolved itself into acts is another matter; and that it habitually resolved itself into the five acts of the editors is doubtful.

The larger rhythm of *Julius Cæsar* can be variously interpreted. The action moves by one impetus, in a barely checked crescendo, to the end of Act III. Cæsar's murder is the theme; the mob provides a recurrent chorus of confusion, and ends, as it has begun, this part of the story. Acts IV and V are given to the murder's retribution; this unifies them. They are martial, more ordered, and, for all the fighting at the end, consistently pitched in a lower key. The five-act division can, however, be defended dramatically; and, if it is valid, it shows us some interesting points of Elizabethan stagecraft. Act I is preparatory and leads up to the conspirators' winning of Brutus, though this itself is kept for the start of Act II. Modern practice would dictate a division after Act I, Sc. ii; for here is a time interval and a change from day to night. But to Shakespeare—or his editor—it would be more important to begin a new act upon a new note, and with the dominant figure of Brutus to impress us. And this we find: each act of the five has a significant and striking beginning, while the ends of the first four all tail away. Act III begins with the ominous

> *Cæsar.* The Ides of March are come.
> *Soothsayer.* Ay, Cæsar, but not gone.

Act IV with the sinister

> *Antony.* These many then shall die; their names are
>   pricked.

Act V with the triumphant

> *Octavius.* Now, Antony, our hopes are answered.

However, it is easy to see why the beginning of an Elizabethan act had to be striking. There was no lowering of the lights, no music, no warning raps, while eyes 'in front' concentrated upon an enigmatic curtain. The actors had to walk on and command the unprepared attention of a probably restless audience, and they needed appropriate material. Equally, to whatever climax of emotion a scene might lead, they would have to walk off again. Therefore neither acts nor scenes, as a rule, end upon a climax.

The play is too strenuous, if not too long, to be acted without at least one pause. It must occur, of course, at the end of Act III. This one should, I personally think, be enough; if pauses are to mean long intervals of talk and distraction, it certainly would be. But if a producer thinks more relief from the strain upon the audience is advisable (his actors do not need it), there is the breathing space at the end of Act II—better not make more of it—and, if that will not suffice, he can pause at the end of Act I. He will be unwise, though, to divide Acts IV and V.

But the form of the play should first be studied in relation to its minor rhythms, for it is in these, in the setting of them one against the other, in their adjustment to the larger rhythm of the main theme, that the liveliness of Shakespeare's stage-craft is to be seen.

The action begins with the entry of the two Tribunes " . . . *and certain commoners over the stage.*" The Roman populace is to play an important part; we have now but a minute's glimpse of it, and in harmless holiday mood.

> Hence! home, you idle creatures, get you home:
> Is this a holiday?

The first lines spoken are a stage-direction for the temper of the scene. It may be that the Globe Theatre ' crowd ' was not much of a crowd, was liable to be unrehearsed and inexact. Line after line scattered through the scene is contrived to describe indirectly how they should look and what they should be expressing. No audience but will accept the suggestion, though the crowd itself be a bit behindhand. Nor need a producer, here or elsewhere, strive to provide a realistically howling mob. The fugleman convention is a part of the convention of the play; reason enough for abiding in it.

Note before we leave this scene how its first full-bodied speech has Pompey for a theme, and what emphasis is given to the first sound of his name. After the chattering prose of the cobbler comes Marullus'

> Wherefore rejoice? What conquest brings he home?
> What tributaries follow him to Rome
> To grace in captive bonds his chariot wheels?
> You blocks, you stones, you worse than senseless things!
> O you hard hearts, you cruel men of Rome,
> Knew you not Pompey?

For Pompey dead is to Cæsar something of what Cæsar dead is to be to Brutus and the rest. And—though Shakespeare naturally does not prejudice an important effect by anticipating it and elaborating its parallel—the name's reiteration throughout the first part of the play has purpose.

A unity is given to these first three acts by the populace; by keeping them constantly in our minds. They are easily persuaded now, controlled and brought to silence :

> They vanish tongue-tied in their guiltiness.

93

The devastation of the third act's end has this mild beginning; a good stroke of dramatic irony.

Against the disorder and inconsequence, Cæsar's processional entrance tells with doubled effect. We are given but a short sight of him, our impression is that he barely pauses on his way. His dominance is affirmed by the simplest means. We hear the name sounded—sounded rather than spoken—seven times in twenty-four lines. The very name is to dominate. It is the cue for Cassius' later outburst:

> Brutus and Cæsar: what should be in that ' Cæsar '?
> Why should that name be sounded more than yours?
> Write them together—yours is as fair a name;
> Sound them, it doth become the mouth as well;
> Weigh them, it is as heavy; conjure with 'em,
> ' Brutus ' will start a spirit as soon as ' Cæsar.'

The procession passes. And now that these opposites, the many-headed and the one, the mob and its moment's idol, have been set in clear contrast before us, the main action may begin.

It is Cassius' passion that chiefly gives tone and colour to the ensuing long duologue. He sets it a swift pace too, which is only checked by Brutus' slow responses; Brutus, lending one ear to his vehement friend, the other keen for the meaning of the distant shouts. Yet, in a sense, it is Cæsar that still holds the stage; in Cassius' rhetoric, in the shouting, in Brutus' strained attention. With his re-entrance, then, there should be no fresh beginning, for the tension created by that first passage across the stage should hardly have been relaxed. Now it increases, that is all. Cæsar pauses a little longer on his way, and with purpose. It is like the passing of a thunder-cloud; presage, in another sort, of the storm by which Nature is to mark his end. To the stately words and trumpet music the procession moves on; and we are left, with the proper shock of contrast, to Casca's acrid and irreverent prose. Now the tension does relax. Then Casca goes, and Brutus and Cassius part with but brief comment on him, without attempting to restore the broken harmony of their thoughts; and Cassius' closing soliloquy, as we have seen, is little more than a perfunctory forwarding of the plot.

" *Thunder and lightning* . . ."

This, the stage empty, would emphasise well enough for the Elizabethans some break of time and place, and a few claps and flashes more might suffice to put a whole storm on record. It does not now suffice Shakespeare. He sets out upon a hundred and sixty-five lines of elaborate verbal scene-painting; in the economy of the plot they really stand for little more. It is not, of course, a merely pictorial effect that he is branding on his audience's imagination. Consider this passage in connection with those appeals of the Chorus in *Henry V :*

> Think when we talk of horses that you see them
> Printing their proud hoofs i' the receiving earth;
> For 'tis your thoughts that now must deck our kings . . .
>
> . . . O! do but think
> You stand upon the rivage and behold
> A city on the inconstant billows dancing;
> For so appears this fleet majestical,
> Holding due course to Harfleur.

All that the listeners were to do for themselves, since the dramatist could not even attempt to do it for them. Here Shakespeare is certainly concerned to picture Rome under the portentous storm, but it is upon the personal episodes he fixes—upon the slave with his burning hand, the

> . . . hundred ghastly women
> Transformed with their fear, who swore they saw
> Men all in fire walk up and down the streets—

upon the marvel of the lion that " glaz'd upon " Casca and " went surly by." And their value to him lies chiefly in their effect upon the emotions of his characters; this is his path to an effect upon ours. He has discovered, in fact, the one dramatic use to which the picturesque can be put in his theatre, and the one and only way of using it. It was not, of course, a discovery sought and made all complete for the occasion. But this is, I think, the first time he brings Nature under such serious contribution. Make another comparison, with the storm scenes in *King Lear*. Set this scene beside those, with their perfect fusion of character and surroundings and their use to the play, and its method seems arbitrary and crude enough. It takes the plot little further. And Cicero is a walking shadow, Cinna a mere convenience ; Casca, unnerved and eloquent, is unrecognisable as the Casca of the previous scene, is turned to a convenience for picturing the storm ; while Cassius only repeats himself, and his rhetoric, dramatically justified before, grows rodomontade. By the end of the hundred and sixty-five lines we have learned that Cicero is cautious, Casca ripe, that things are moving fast with Cinna and the rest, that Brutus must be won. At his best Shakespeare could have achieved this in fifty lines or less and given us the storm into the bargain.

The contrasting calm of the next act's beginning is an appropriate setting for Brutus, the stoic, the man of conscience and gentle mind. The play's scheme now opens out and grows clear, for Brutus takes his allotted and fatal place among his fellows as moral dictator. To his dominance is due the scene's coldness and rigidity, though the unity of tone gives it dignity and its circumstance alone would make effective drama. Incidental things give it vitality and such colour as it needs; the coming and going of the sleepy boy, the knocking without, the striking of the clock followed by those three short echoing speeches. It all stays to the end rather static than dynamic; for high-mindedly as Brutus may harangue his "gentle friends," fervently as they may admire him, there is never, now or later, the spontaneous sympathy between them that alone gives life to a cause. The ultimate as well as the immediate tragedy is in the making.

The scene with Portia is the due sequel. Even from her he holds aloof. He loves her; but the more he loves her the less he can confide in her. Even the avowal of his love is wrung from him in a sort of agony. And Portia's own tragedy is in the making here. In her spent patience with his silence we might well divine the impatience at his absence which was to be her death. We may question why, after a vibrant climax, Shakespeare so lowers the tension for the scene's end. Caius Ligarius' coming will surely thrust Portia and this more intimate Brutus to the background of our remembrance. There are two answers at

97

least. The play's main action must not only be
carried on, but it must seem now to be hurried on,
and Brutus, his philosophic reserve once broken,
must be shown precipitate.[1] For another answer;
the Caius Ligarius episode keeps the scenes
between Brutus and Portia, Cæsar and Calpurnia
apart. It would discount the second to bring it
on the heels of the first.

Thunder and lightning herald the next scene's
beginning; the purpose of its repetition is plain
enough. The mood wrought in us by the storm
must be restored; and in a moment comes
Calpurnia's speech, which is a very echo of Casca's
description of the signs and portents. Cæsar,
rocklike at first against the pleadings of his wife,
wavers from his love for her and yields to Decius'
friendliness and flattery, reinforced by the throng-
ing in of the rest, looking, as Brutus bid them look,
so " fresh and merrily." It is good preparation
for the catastrophe, the sudden livening of the
scene with this group of resolute, cheerful men.
Besides, might not the slim Decius have over-
reached himself but for their coming? Cæsar was
no fool, and Calpurnia would be apt to every sort
of suspicion. But the friendly faces disperse the

[1] Here, incidentally, is an instance of an effect made for
its own sake and in the confidence that no awkward questions will be asked. The immediate suggestion is that
Brutus and Ligarius go straight to the conspirators, thence
with them to Cæsar and the Senate House. It is left mere
suggestion and not further defined, for Portia has to be told
of the conspiracy " by and by," and, when we next see her,
the suggestion—still mere suggestion—is that she has been
told. But Shakespeare knows that no questions will be
asked as long as the effects are spaced out, if distractions
intervene and positive contradiction is avoided.

last clouds of the ominous night. Cassius is not here. It is Brutus, the irreproachable Brutus, who gives tone to the proceeding. Does he, even at this moment, feel himself

> . . . arm'd so strong in honesty

that he can meet Cæsar's magnanimity without flinching? Is it only ague that makes Caius Ligarius shake as Cæsar presses his hand? And that nothing of tragic irony may be wanting—

> Good friends, go in, and taste some wine with me,
> And we, like friends, will straightway go together.

The sacrament of hospitality and trust! It is a supreme effect, economised in words, fully effective only in action. And for an instance of Shakespeare's dramatic judgment, of his sense of balance between an immediate effect and the play's continuing purpose, of his power, in striking one note, to strike the ruthlessly right one, take the two lines with which Brutus, lagging back, ends the scene:

> That every like is not the same, O Cæsar!
> The heart of Brutus yearns to think upon.

Not that a pun or a quibble of words necessarily struck an Elizabethan, as it strikes us, for a thing essentially trifling. But it takes a Brutus to find refuge in a quibbling thought at such a moment, and in his own grief for his victim.

Cæsar is now ringed by the conspirators, the daggers are ready, and the two scenes that follow are to hold and prolong the suspense till they strike.[1] Artemidorus, with his paper and its com-

[1] Unless every clearance of the stage is to mark a division of scenes, they are, of course, but one. No particular change of location is implied. Upon the question of the act division here, see also page 91.

8

ment, may seem unduly dry and detached. But the solitary anonymous figure comes as a relief and contrast to that significant group, and against that wrought emotion his very detachment tells. It contrasts too with Portia's tremulous intimate concern. The act's end here—if it is to mean a short empty pause while the audience stay seated and expectant, not an interval of talk and move-ment—will have value. The blow is about to fall, and in silence suspense is greatest. We draw breath for the two long scenes that form the centre section of the play.

Trumpets sound, the stage fills. Cæsar comes again as we saw him go, still circled by these friends, confident, outwardly serene. The trum-pets silent, we hear another prelude, of two voices, the one ringing clear, the other pallidly echoing.

Cæsar. The Ides of March are come.
The Soothsayer. Ay, Cæsar, but not gone.

Then follows a little scuffle of voices, a quick shifting and elbowing in the group round Cæsar as the petitions are thrust forward and aside, and once again that fivefold iteration of the potent name. For all the ceremony, nerves are on edge. Cæsar goes forward to be greeted by the Senators and to mount his state. Now comes a passage of eighteen lines. Toneless it has to be. In the group of speakers there is hardly a movement; they must measure even their glances. Popilius Lena's threading his way through them is startling in itself. Yet on this monotone the whole gamut of the conspiracy's doubts, fears and desperation is run. Its midway sentence is the steely

Cassius, be constant

with which Brutus marks his mastery of the rest.
Cæsar is seated. His

> Are we all ready?

turns the whole concourse to him. Some few of
them are ready indeed. And now, in terms of
deliberate rhetoric, Shakespeare again erects
before us the Colossus that is to be overthrown.
Then in a flash the blow falls. Butchered by
Casca, sacrificed by Brutus—these two doings
of the same deed are marked and kept apart
—and with no more words about it, Cæsar lies
dead.

Remark that we are now only a quarter of the
way through the scene; further, that the play's
whole action so far has been a preparation for this
crisis. Yet, with dead Cæsar lying there, Shakespeare will contrive to give us such fresh interest in
the living that, with no belittling of the catastrophe,
no damping-down nor desecration of our emotions,
our minds will be turned forward still. This is a
great technical achievement. He might well
have shirked the full attempt and have wound up
the scene with its next seventy lines or so. But
then could the play ever have recovered strength
and impetus? As it is, by the long scene's end our
concern for Cæsar is lost in our expectations of the
Forum. The producer must note carefully how
this is brought about, lest even the minor means to
it miscarry.

The mainspring of the renewed action will lie,
of course, in the creation of Antony. We may call
it so; for, as we saw, he has been cunningly kept,
in person and by reference, an ineffectual figure
so far. But now both in person and by reference,

by preparation, by contrast, Shakespeare brings him to a sudden overwhelming importance.

We have the helter-skelter of the moment after Cæsar's fall; Brutus is the only figure of authority and calm. Old Publius stands trembling and dumb; Antony, that slight man, has fled, and the conspirators seem confounded by their very success. Before, then, they face the Rome they have saved from tyranny, let them make themselves one again, not in false courage—if Rome is ungrateful they must die—but in high principle that fears not death. Let them sign themselves ritual brothers—and in whose blood but Cæsar's?

> Stoop, Romans, stoop,
> And let us bathe our hands in Cæsar's blood
> Up to the elbows, and besmear our swords:
> Then walk we forth, even to the market-place,
> And waving our red weapons o'er our heads,
> Let's all cry, " Peace, freedom, and liberty."

We need not doubt Brutus' deep sincerity for a moment.

> Fates, we will know your pleasures.
> That we shall die we know; 'tis but the time
> And drawing days out, that men stand upon.

This is the man of principle at his noblest. But what else than savage mockery is Casca's

> Why, he that cuts off twenty years of life
> Cuts off so many years of fearing death?

And does Brutus, the rapt ideologue, perceive it? Into the sophistical trap he walks.

> Grant that, and then is death a benefit:
> So are we Cæsar's friends, that have abridg'd
> His time of fearing death.

And he anoints himself devotedly.   Then Cassius,
febrile, infatuate:

> Stoop, then, and wash.   How many ages hence
> Shall this our lofty scene be acted o'er,
> In states unborn and accents yet unknown!

Brutus echoes him as well.   And by this last
daring and doubly dramatic stroke, Shakespeare
reminds us that we are ideal spectators of these
men and the event, having vision and prevision
too.   Comment is forbidden the playwright, but
here is the effect of it contrived.   For as we
look and listen we hear the verdict of the ages
echoing.   In this imperfect world, it would seem,
one can be too high-minded, too patriotic, too
virtuous altogether.   And then the commonest
thing, if it be rooted firm, may trip a man to
his ruin.   So these exalted gentlemen, led by their
philosophic patriot, are stopped on their way—
by the arrival of a servant.[1]

This is the play's turning-point.   And, if but
pictorially, could a better be contrived?   On the
one side the group of triumphant and powerful
men; on the other, suddenly appearing, a humble,
anonymous messenger.

> Thus, Brutus, did my master bid me kneel;
> Thus did Mark Antony bid me fall down;
> And, being prostrate, thus he bade me say . . .

And so aptly and literally does he represent his
master that Brutus, with this chance to test the

[1] For an excellent analysis of this passage see MacCullum's
Shakespeare's Roman Plays, quoted by Furness.   And for the
effect of the servant's entrance see, as before noted, R. G.
Moulton's *Shakespeare as Dramatic Artist*.

smooth words apart from their deviser, might, we should suppose, take warning. But it is Brutus who is infatuate now. It is not, as with Cassius, passions that blind him, but principles. He has done murder for an ideal. Not to credit his adversaries, in turn, with the highest motives would be unworthy, would seem sheer hypocrisy. And Antony's message is baited with an uncanny knowledge of the man.

> Brutus is noble, wise, valiant, and honest;
> Cæsar was mighty, bold, royal, and loving:
> Say I love Brutus, and I honour him;
> Say I fear'd Cæsar, honour'd him, and lov'd him.

Wisdom and honesty, valour and love, honour and again honour; Brutus will harp on the very words in his own apology. It is Cassius, with his vengeance fulfilled and his passions gratified, who now sees clear, knowing his Antony as truly as Antony knows his Brutus. His

> . . . misgiving still
> Falls shrewdly to the purpose.

But he lacks authority to lead.

Then follows the revelation of Antony, in his verbal duel with the conspirators; his devoted rhapsody over Cæsar's body; and the swift foresight of the passage with Octavius' servant. It is to be noted that the beginning of the scene in the Forum tags dramatically not to the end of this but to the earlier departure of Brutus and the others. Hence, perhaps, the short opening in verse and Brutus' echoing of his last spoken line,

> Prepare the body then and follow us,

with

> Then follow me, and give me audience, friends.

104

Once he is in the pulpit we have a sharp change to prose.

Editor after editor has condemned Brutus' speech as poor and ineffective, and most of them have then proceeded to justify Shakespeare for making it so. It is certainly not meant to be ineffective, for it attains its end in convincing the crowd. Whether it is poor oratory must be to some extent a matter of taste. Personally, accepting its form as one accepts the musical convention of a fugue, I find that it stirs me deeply. I prefer it to Antony's. It wears better. It is very noble prose. But we must, of course, consider it first as a part of the setting out of Brutus' character. Nothing—if the speech itself does not—suggests him to us as a poor speaker; nor, at this moment of all others, would he fail himself. But we know the sort of appeal he would, deliberately if not tempera- mentally, avoid. Shakespeare has been accused, too, of bias against the populace. But is it so? He had no illusions about them. As a popular dramatist he faced their inconstant verdict day by day, and came to write for a better audience than he had. He allows Brutus no illusions, certainly.

> Only be patient till we have appeas'd
> The multitude, beside themselves with fear.

This is the authentic voice of your republican aristocrat, who is at no pains, either, to disguise his disdain.

> Be patient till the last.
> Romans, countrymen and lovers! hear me for my
> cause; and be silent, that you may hear.

For the tone belies the words; nor is such a rapping on the desk for ' quiet, please ' the obvious way into the affections of the heady crowd. He concedes nothing to their simplicity.

> Censure me in your wisdom, and awake your senses, that you may be the better judge.

But the compliment, one fears, is paid less to them than to his own intellectual pride. It is wasted in any case, if we may judge by the third and fourth citizens.

> Let him be Cæsar,
>   Cæsar's better parts
> Shall be crown'd in Brutus.

He has won them; not by what he has said, in spite of it, rather; but by what he is. The dramatic intention, and the part the crowd plays in it, is surely plain. Men in the mass do not think, they feel. They are as biddable as children, and as sensitive to suggestion. Mark Antony is to make it plainer.

Antony has entered, and stands all friendless by Cæsar's bier. Brutus descends, the dialogue shifting from prose to easy verse as he shakes free of the enthusiasm, and departs alone. His austere renouncing of advantage should show us how truly alone.

Antony makes no glib beginning; he protests, indeed, that he has nothing to say. He tries this opening and that, is deprecatory, apologetic.

>   The noble Brutus
> Hath told you Cæsar was ambitious.
> If it were so, it was a grievous fault,
> And grievously hath Cæsar answered it.

But he is deftly feeling his way by help of a few platitudes to his true opening, and alert for a first response. He senses one, possibly, upon his

> He was my friend, faithful and just to me

—for that was a human appeal. But he knows better than to presume on a success; he returns to his praise of the well-bepraised Brutus. He embellishes the tune with two grace-notes, one of sentiment, the other of greed. More praise of Brutus, and yet more! But the irony of this will out, and he checks himself. Irony is a tricky weapon with an audience uncertain still. Nor will too much nice talk about honour serve him; that sort of thing leaves men cold. A quick turn gives us

> I speak not to disprove what Brutus spoke;
> But here I am to speak what I do know,

and, by the hammering monosyllables of the last line, he is warming to his work, and feels his hearers warming to him.

One may so analyse the speech throughout and find it a triumph of effective cleverness. The cheapening of the truth, the appeals to passion, the perfect carillon of flattery, cajolery, mockery and pathos, swinging to a magnificent tune, all serve to make it a model of what popular oratory should be. In a school for demagogues its critical analysis might well be an item in every examination paper. That is one view of it. By another, there is nothing in it calculated or false. Antony feels like this; and, on these occasions, he never lets his thoughts belie his feelings, that is all. And he knows, without stopping to think, what the common thought and feeling will be, where reason and sentiment will touch bottom—and if it be a muddy bottom what matter!—because he is himself, as we said, the common man raised to the highest power. So, once in touch with his audience, he can hardly go wrong.

How easy he makes things for them! No abstract arguments:

> But here's a parchment with the seal of Cæsar.
> I found it in his closet, 'tis his will.

We pass now, however, to a less ingenuous, more ingenious, phase of the achievement. Those—it is strange there should be any—who range themselves with the mob and will see in Antony no more than the plain blunt man of his own painting, have still to account for this slim manipulator of Cæsar's will that Shakespeare paints. It is tempting, no doubt, to make men dance to your tune when the thing is done so easily. When they stand, open-eared and open-mouthed, how resist stuffing them with any folly that comes handy? And as there is no limit, it would seem, to their folly and credulity, greed and baseness, why not turn it all to good account—one's own account? Antony is not the man, at any rate, to turn aside from such temptation. Is he less of a demagogue that Cæsar's murder is his theme, and vengeance for it his cause? Does poetic eloquence make demagogy less vicious—or, by chance, more? Shakespeare's Antony would not be complete without this juggling with Cæsar's will.

What so impresses the unlearned as the sight of some document? He does not mean to read it. They are Cæsar's heirs. There, he never meant to let that slip! Trick after trick of the oratorical trade follows. The provocative appeal to the seething crowd's self-control tagged to the flattery of their generous hearts, the play with the mantle, which they " all do know," that soft touch of the " summer's evening " when Cæsar first put it on! Self-interest well salted with senti-ment, what better bait can there be? Much may be done with a blood-stained bit of cloth!

> Through this the well-beloved Brutus stabbed;
> And as he pluck'd his cursèd steel away,
> Mark how the blood of Cæsar followed it,
> As rushing out of doors, to be resolved
> If Brutus so unkindly knocked, or no.

If our blood were still cold the simile might sound ridiculous, but it thrills us now.

> That was the most unkindest cut of all;
> For when the noble Cæsar saw him stab,
> Ingratitude, more strong than traitors' arms,
> Quite vanquished him: then burst his mighty heart;
> And, in his mantle muffling up his face,
> Even at the base of Pompey's statua,
> Which all the while ran blood, great Cæsar fell.

How fine it sounds! How true, therefore, by the standards of popular oratory, it is! There is poetic truth, certainly, in that ingratitude; and as for Pompey's statue, if it did not actually run blood, it might well have done.

> O! what a fall was there, my countrymen;
> Then I, and you, and all of us fell down,
> Whilst bloody treason flourished over us.
> O! now you weep, and I perceive you feel
> The dint of pity. . . .

What were Brutus' tributes to their wisdom com-pared to this? Antony has won their tears, and has

but to seal his success by showing them the very
body of Cæsar, and to endorse it with

> Good friends, sweet friends, let me not stir you up
> To such a sudden flood of mutiny.
> They that have done this deed are honourable . . .

for irony is a potent weapon now.

The peroration is masterly, a compendium
of excitement. We have again the false restraint
from passion, the now triumphant mockery of
those honourable men, of their wisdom, their
good reasons and their private grief; again, the
plain blunt man's warning against such oratorical
snares as the subtle Brutus set; and it is all
rounded off with magnificent rhythm, the recurrent
thought and word flung like a stone from a sling.

> . . . but were I Brutus,
> And Brutus Antony, there were an Antony
> Would ruffle up your spirits, and put a tongue
> In every wound of Cæsar that should move
> The stones of Rome to rise and mutiny.

And to what end? To the routing of the conspirators from Rome, truly. A good counter-
stroke. But the first victim of Antony's eloquence,
as Shakespeare takes care to show us, is the
wretched Cinna the poet, who has had nothing to
do with Cæsar's murder at all.[1] The mob tear
him limb from limb, as children tear a rag doll.
Nor does knowledge of his innocence hinder them.

> Truly, my name is Cinna.
> Tear him to pieces, he's a conspirator.
> I am Cinna, the poet, I am Cinna the poet.

---

[1] A scene which the average modern producer takes great
care to cut.

> Tear him for his bad verses, tear him for his bad verses.
>
> I am not Cinna the conspirator.
>
> It is no matter, his name's Cinna; pluck but his name out of his heart and turn him going.

Well, we have had Antony's fine oratory; and we may have been, and should have been, stirred by it. But if we have not at the same time watched him, and ourselves, with a discerning eye, and listened as well with a keener ear, the fault is none of Shakespeare's. He draws no moral, does not wordily balance the merits of this cause against that. He is content to compose for the core of his play, with an artist's enjoyment, with an artist's conscience in getting the balance true, this ironic picture; and, finally, to set against the high tragedy of the murder of Cæsar a poor poetaster's wanton slaughter.

The beginning of the fourth act sets against the calculations of the conspirators the arithmetic of the new masters of Rome.

> These many, then, shall die; their names are pricked.

It is an admirably done scene, of but fifty lines all told, giving an actor, with just twenty-two words, material for Lepidus (the feat would seem impossible, but Shakespeare manages it; and so can an actor, rightly chosen and given scope), giving us Octavius, showing us yet another Antony, and outlining the complete gospel of political success. Brutus and Cassius, its finish informs us, are levying powers. We are shown them straightway at the next scene's beginning, and from now to the play's end its action runs a straight road.

Drum. Enter Brutus.

The philosopher has turned general. He is graver, more austere than ever.

> Your master, Pindarus,
> In his own change, or by ill officers
> Hath given me some worthy cause to wish
> Things done undone. . . .

But he says it as one who would say that nothing, be it big or little, can ever be undone. We hear a "*Low march within,*" congruous accompaniment to the sombre voice. It heralds Cassius.

Enter Cassius and his Powers.

Cassius. Stand, ho.
Brutus. Stand, ho.
First Soldier. Stand.
Second Soldier. Stand.
Third Soldier. Stand.

The voices echo back, the drum-beats cease, the armed men face each other, silent a moment.[1]

This long scene—the play's longest—thus begun, is dominated by Brutus and attuned in the main to his mood. Now the mood of the good man in adversity may well make for monotony and gloom; but Shakespeare is alert to avoid this, and so must producer and actors be. We have the emotional elaboration of the quarrel, the

[1] The chorus in *Henry V* could not apologise enough for the theatre's failure to show armies in being. But by a little music, this little cunning of speech and action, and a bold acceptance of convention, these "ciphers to this great account" can be made to work well enough upon the "imaginary forces" of the audience.

eccentric interlude of the poet as preparation for the sudden drop to the deep still note struck by the revelation of Portia's death; next comes the steady talk of fighting plans (note the smooth verse), then the little stir with which the council breaks up and the simple preparations for the night. Varro and Claudius are brought in, so that their sleep, as well as the boy's, may throw the calm, wakeful figure of Brutus into relief. The tune and its lapsing brings a hush, we can almost hear the leaves of the book rustle as they are turned. Then the ghost appears; the tense few moments of its presence have been well prepared. The scene's swift ending is good stage-craft too. Lucius' protesting treble, the deeper voices of the soldiers all confused with sleep, the dissonance and sharp interchange break and disperse the ominous spell for Brutus and for us. And the last words look forward.[1]

The last act of *Julius Cæsar* has been most inconsiderately depreciated. Nothing, certainly, will make it effective upon the modern ' realistic ' stage, but we can hardly blame Shakespeare for that. He writes within the conventions of his own theatre, and he here takes the fullest advantage

[1] " Sleep again, Lucius," would point, if nothing else did, to the drawing together of the curtains of the inner stage upon the scene. Where Varro and Claudius have been lying is a question. They enter, of course, upon the main stage. Brutus apparently points to the inner stage with " Lie in my tent and sleep." They offer to keep watch where they are, *i.e.* by the door. I am inclined to think that they lie down there, too. This would not only make the business with the ghost better, but it would bring the scene's final piece of action upon the centre stage and give it breadth and importance.

of them. He begins by bringing the rival armies, led by their generals, face to face.

Enter Octavius, Antony and their army . . .
Drum. Enter Brutus, Cassius and their army.

Brutus. They stand and would have parley.
Cassius. Stand fast, Titinius; we must out and talk.
Octavius. Mark Antony, shall we give sign of battle?
Antony. No, Cæsar, we will answer on their charge.
Make forth; the generals would have some words.

This to the Elizabethans was a commonplace of stagecraft. Before scenery which paints realistically some defined locality, it must needs look absurd. But, the simpler convention accepted, Shakespeare sets for his audience a wider and more significant scene than any the scenic theatre can compass. And, confronting the fighters, he states the theme, so to speak, of the play's last event, and gives it value, importance and dignity.

The whole act is constructed with the greatest care, each detail has its purpose and effect. But we must dismiss, even from our memories if possible, the *Scene* ii, *The same, The Field of Battle*; and *Scene* iii, *Another Part of the Field*, of the editors. What happens to begin with is this. Antony, Octavius and their powers departed, the talk between Brutus and Cassius over—it is their third and last, and a chill quiet talk, for they feel they are under the shadow of defeat—the stage is left empty. Then the silence is broken by the clattering *alarum*, the symbol of a battle begun. Then back comes Brutus, and a very different Brutus.[1]

[1] Every scene's ending involves an empty stage. But the difference of effect between the entry of fresh characters to begin the next and the re-entry of the same character after a necessary pause, but in an altered mood, will be appreciable.

114

> Ride, ride, Messala, ride, and give these bills
> Unto the legions on the other side.

Now a *Loud Alarum*, which his voice must drown.

> Let them set on at once, for I perceive
> But cold demeanour in Octavius' wing,
> And sudden push gives them the overthrow.
> Ride, ride, Messala: let them all come down.

And he is gone as he came. It is a most stirringly dramatic effect. But it cannot be achieved if tension is relaxed and attention dissipated by the shifting of scenery, or by any superfluous embroidering of the action.

Remark further that to follow the course of the battle an audience must listen keenly, and they must be able to concentrate their minds on the speakers. When the defeat of Cassius is imminent, when Titinius tells him:

> O Cassius! Brutus gave the word too early,
> Who, having some advantage on Octavius,
> Took it too eagerly: his soldiers fell to spoil,
> Whilst we by Antony are all enclos'd,

the situation is made clear enough. But if we do not master it at this moment, the rest of the scene and its drama will go for next to nothing.

Now we have Cassius grasping the ensign he has seized from the coward who was running away with it (and, being Cassius, not content with that, he has killed the man), the very ensign the birds of ill omen had hovered over; and he makes as if to plant it defiantly, conspicuously in the ground.

> This hill is far enough . . .

His death is of a piece with his whole reckless life. He kills himself because he will not wait

another minute to verify the tale his bondman tells
him of Titinius' capture. He ends passionately
and desperately—but still grasping his standard.
Even at this moment he is as harsh to Pindarus
as Brutus is gentle to his boy Lucius and the
bondman who serves him.

> Come hither, sirrah:
> In Parthia did I take thee prisoner;
> And then I swore thee, saving of thy life,
> That whatsoever I did bid thee do,
> Thou shouldst attempt it.

His last words are as bare and ruthless.

> Cæsar, thou art reveng'd
> Even with the sword that kill'd thee.

Pindarus' four lines that follow may seem frigid
and formal. But we need a breathing space before
we face the tragically ironic return of Titinius
radiant with good news. The stagecraft of this
entrance, as of others like it, belongs, we must
remember, to the Elizabethan theatre, with its
doors at the back, and its distance for an actor to
advance, attention full on him. Entrance from
the wing of a conventional scenic stage will be
quite another matter.

Messala. It is but change, Titinius; for Octavius
 Is overthrown by noble Brutus' power,
 As Cassius' legions are by Antony.
Titinius. These tidings will well comfort Cassius.
Messala. Where did you leave him?
Titinius.   All disconsolate,
 With Pindarus his bondman, on this hill.
Messala. Is that not he that lies along the ground?
Titinius He lies not like the living. O my heart!
Messala. Is not that he?
Titinius.   No, this was he, Messala,
 But Cassius is no more.

Stage direction is embodied in dialogue. We have the decelerated arrival telling of relief from strain, the glance around the seemingly empty place; then the sudden swift single-syllabled line and its repetition, Titinius' dart forward, Messala's graver question, the dire finality of the answer.

We come to Titinius' death; and it is a legitimate query why, with two suicides to provide for, Shakespeare burdened himself with this third. The episode itself may have attracted him; the soldier crowning his dead chief with the garland of victory; then, as the innocent cause of his death, set not to survive it.[1] The death speech is fine, and the questioning sentences that begin it whip it to great poignancy. But neither here nor anywhere, we must admit, does Shakespeare show full understanding of the ' Roman's part,' and the strange faith that let him play it. His Romans go to their deaths stoically enough, but a little stockily too. Hamlet, later, will find the question arguable, and Macbeth will think a man a fool not to die fighting. Brutus and Cassius and Titinius, it is true, could hardly be made to argue the point here. But there is an abruptness and a sameness, and a certain emptiness, in the manner of these endings.

Another and technically a stronger reason for adding Titinius to the suicides, is that it is above all important Brutus' death should not come as an anticlimax to Cassius'. This episode helps provide against that danger, and the next scene makes escape from it sure.

The bodies are carried out in procession with

[1] Shakespeare finds this more clearly put in Plutarch than he leaves it in the play.

due dignity, and again the empty stage keys us to expectancy. Then

Alarum. Enter Brutus, Messala, Cato, Lucilius and Flavius. Enter soldiers and fight.

It is a noisy mellay; so confused, that though we hear the voices of the leaders from its midst, Brutus disappears unnoticed. The scene has its touch of romance in young Cato's death, its dash of intrigue in Lucilius' trick. If these things are given value in performance, they knot up effectively the weakening continuity of theme, which, by its slacking, would leave the death of Brutus and the play's end a fag-end instead of a full close.

Yet the effects of the last scene are in themselves most carefully elaborated. Hard upon the clattering excitement of the fight, and the flattering magnanimity of the triumphant Antony, comes into sight this little group of beaten and exhausted men, the torch-light flickering on their faces.

Brutus. Come, poor remains of friends, rest on this rock.
Clitus. Statilius show'd the torch-light; but, my lord,
He came not back: he is or ta'en or slain.
Brutus. Sit thee down, Clitus: slaying is the word;
It is a deed in fashion . . .

They throw themselves down hopelessly; to wait —for what!—and to brood in a silence which Brutus hardly breaks by his whisper, first to Clitus, next to Dardanius. Then he paces apart while the two watch him and themselves whisper of the dreadful demand he made. He calls on Volumnius next, to find in him, not hope, only the instinctive human reluctance to admit an end. But his own end—and he knows and desires it—is here. Threatening low alarums vibrate beneath his calm, colourless speech. His followers cry to him to save himself, and a like cry from far off pierces that still insistent alarum, and they echo it again. Well, these men have life and purpose left in them; let them go. He praises and humours their loyalty. But, at his command, they leave him. The end is very near.

But Shakespeare himself is not yet at the end of his resources, nor of his constant care to weave the action in a living texture, to give the least of its figures life. What, till this moment, do we know about Strato? He makes his first appearance in the battle; he is Brutus' body servant, it seems. A thick-skinned sort of fellow; while the others counted the cost of their ruin, he had fallen asleep. Twelve lines or so (he himself speaks just seven) not only make a living figure of him but keep Brutus self-enlightening to the last. For the very last note struck out of this stoic, whose high principles could not stop short of murder, is one of gentleness.

> *Brutus.* I prithee, Strato, stay thou by thy lord:
> Thou art a fellow of a good respect;
> Thy life hath had some smatch of honour in it:
> Hold then my sword, and turn away thy face,
> While I do run upon it. Wilt thou, Strato?
> *Strato.* Give me your hand first: fare you well, my lord.
> *Brutus.* Farewell, good Strato . . .

The man's demand for a handshake, the master's response to it;—how much of Shakespeare's greatness lies in these little things, and in the love of his art that never found them too little for his care! Then Brutus closes his account.

> Cæsar, now be still;
> I kill'd not thee with half so good a will.

In silence on both sides the thing is done. Nor
does Strato stir while the loud alarum and retreat
are sounded; he does not even turn at the
conquerors' approach—Antony, Octavius, and the
already reconciled Messala and Lucilius, who only
see by the light of the torches this solitary figure
standing there.

Nor have we even yet reached the play's formal
close, the ceremonial lifting of the body, the
apostrophe to the dead, and that turning towards
the living future which the conditions of the
Elizabethan stage inevitably and happily pre-
scribed. Chief place is given here, as we have
noted, to Octavius, Cæsar's heir and—if Shakespeare may have had it in mind—the conqueror-
to-be of his fellow-conqueror. But we have first a
bitter-sweet exchange between Strato and Messala.
They—and they know it—are commoner clay than
their master who lies here; no vain heroism for
them. Next Antony speaks, and makes sportsman-
like amends to his dead enemy.

The play is a masterpiece of Elizabethan stagecraft, and the last act, from this point of view,
especially remarkable; but only by close analysis
can its technical virtues be made plain. Within
the powerful ease of its larger rhythm, the constant,
varied ebb and flow and interplay of purpose,
character and event give it richness of dramatic
life, and us the sense of its life-likeness.

STAGING AND COSTUME

No difficulties arise—why should they?—in
fitting the play to such a stage as we suppose
Shakespeare's at the Globe to have been; at most

a few questions must be answered as to the use of the inner stage for this scene or that. Further, the resources of this stage, its adapting of space and time to the playwright's convenience, are so fully exploited that the producer who means to use another had better be very careful he does not lose more than he gains.

Act I can be played wholly on the main stage.

Act II. " *Enter Brutus in his Orchard*," says the Folio. This looks like a discovery upon the inner stage. There will certainly be the dramatic effect of contrast, after the feverish excursions through the night of storm, in our seeing Brutus, a chief subject of them, sitting in the contained quiet of his garden. The opening speech, by which, as a rule, Shakespeare paints us the aspect of his scene if he wants to, gives in its tone and in its interspersed silences both the solitary man and the stillness after the storm.

> What, Lucius! ho!
> I cannot, by the progress of the stars,
> Give guess how near to day. Lucius, I say!
> I would it were my fault to sleep so soundly.
> When, Lucius, when! Awake, I say! what, Lucius!

Lucius may enter directly upon the inner stage. Brutus might speak his first soliloquy still sitting there. It is possible that at the Globe he did not, the actor there may have needed a better point of vantage for such an intimately reflective passage.[1] The knocking would almost certainly be heard beyond one of the main stage doors,

[1] I write this very much under correction. But I believe that only experiment will tell us what could and could not be made effective upon the inner and upper stages at the Globe.

121

through which the conspirators would come, for the scene's general action must be upon the main stage without a doubt. For the scene which follows the traverse must, one would suppose, be closed, to hide whatever properties suggested Brutus' garden. But *Enter Cæsar in his nightgown*, even though he enter upon the main stage, will sufficiently suggest an interior. And the main stage will serve for the rest of the second act.

We should note the space-freedom Shakespeare assumes. "Here will I stand," says Artemidorus, "till Cæsar pass along"; but, speaking five lines more, he goes off, to reappear with the crowd that follows Cæsar. And Act III begins with a most significant instance of it. The inner stage is disclosed and Cæsar's 'state' is set there. Cæsar, the conspirators, the Senators and the populace enter upon the main stage. Cassius speaks to Artemidorus:

> What! urge you your petitions in the street?
> Come to the Capitol.

Eighteen lines later we have

> *Cæsar.* Are we all ready? what is now amiss
>   That Cæsar and his Senate must redress?
> *Metellus.* Most high, most mighty, and most puissant
>   Cæsar,
>   Metellus Cimber throws before thy seat
>   An humble heart——

Nothing more complicated has occurred than Cæsar and the Senators taking their places, while the crowd disperses and the conspirators regroup themselves, so that the 'state' becomes the centre of attraction—and we are in the Senate-house. Later, Cæsar must fall and lie dead in a most conspicuous position upon the main stage; still later provision must be made—as it is—for removing the body.

For the following scene the traverse is closed and the upper stage is used for the pulpit. Moreover, the dialogue tells us, to a second or so, the time it takes to ascend and come down.

The first scene of Act IV might, but need not, be played in relation to the inner stage.[1] The second and third scenes, which are not divided in the Folio—which are indeed conspicuously left undivided there—present us with another

[1] I think that scenes were more often played 'in relation to' the inner stage than consistently within its boundaries; that is to say, the actors, having gained the effect of a discovery, would be apt to advance upon the main stage, where their movements would be less cramped, where they would be in closer touch with the audience and certainly in a better position to hold an unruly audience. I see this happening in the scene in Brutus' garden, and possibly in this scene. There are signs of such a treatment, too, of the scene in Brutus' tent. When he asks Lucius, "Where is thy instrument?" "Here in the tent" is the answer, not a simple "I have it here." When he calls in Varro and Claudius, he says, "I pray you, Sirs, lie in my tent and sleep." It sounds very much like people upon the main stage indicating the inner stage with a gesture. Certain things, the study of the map, the playing of the lute, the reading by the taper's light, show, of course, the use of furniture. This would probably be set and left upon the inner stage, though it would be advantageous to have it placed as near the traverse-line as possible, and actors, using it, would be constantly passing the line. And, speaking generally, one need not suppose that the Elizabethan actor ever saw the division between inner stage and main stage as a fixed boundary, nor that the Elizabethan audience had cultivated such a sense of locality that they questioned its crossing and re-crossing or even asked themselves at certain ambiguous moments where exactly the characters were meant to be. The main effect and its dramatic purpose were reckoned with; whatever assisted this was allowed.

significant instance of space-freedom, and of Shakespeare's ready use of the conventions which belong to it.[1] We have

Enter Brutus, Lucilius and the Army. . . .

The editors cannot leave this alone. " *The Army* " becomes " *and soldiers.* "[2] This falsifies Shakespeare's intention. By " *the Army* " he does not mean a few casual soldiers, he means the integral group of followers, in some uniform possibly, and with banner, drum and trumpet, which in Elizabethan stage convention personified and symbolised an army entire. Later, after a *low march within* comes

Enter Cassius and his Powers.

And much the same thing is meant. The effect to be gained is of the spaciousness and order of armies in the field in contrast with that chaos of the market-place; and it is as important as an explanatory scene would be.

And what really occurs where modern editors mark a change of scene?

Brutus. Let us not wrangle : bid them move away ;
   Then in my tent, Cassius, enlarge your griefs,
   And I will give you audience.
Cassius.   Pindarus,
   Bid our commanders lead their charges off
   A little from this ground.
Brutus. Lucius, do you the like, and let no man
   Come to our tent till we have done our conference.

Exeunt. Manet Brutus and Cassius.

---

[1] The play in the Folio (and there are no Quartos) is one of those which start bravely with 'Actus Primus Scaena Prima' and then pay no further attention to scene-division at all. I refer in my enumeration of scenes to the current modern editions, which are, however, in this particular most misleading to the student of the Elizabethan stage and of Shakespeare the dramatist.

[2] Capel did no worse than change it to "*Forces.*"

Then, without more ado, with no slackening of tension nor waste of this excellently ominous preparation, the intimate wrangle begins. The stagecraft is plain enough. The symbolised armies, with their banners and drums, go off; and either the traverse is now drawn, disclosing the tent furniture, in which case Brutus and Cassius have but to place themselves in relation to it for the scene to be effectively changed; or it is as possible that the traverse has been open from the beginning and that the removal of the 'armies' and the re-orientation of the chief actors were felt to be change enough. This would repeat the mechanics of the Senate-house scene (but it would, of course, forbid an immediately previous use of the inner stage for Antony and Octavius).

We come to Act V, which must be envisaged as a whole. The locality is a battle-field. We have still the symbolical armies. The scenes are divided by alarums. The conventions, in fact, are all accepted. The upper stage is used, for a moment, as the high point of a hill.

Go, Pindarus, get higher on that hill,

says Cassius, and six lines later the direction reads

Pindarus above.

The only sign of use of the inner stage is for the scene beginning,

Brutus. Come, poor remains of friends, rest on this rock.

Brutus and his friends may need something better to sit upon than the floor. It need be no realistic rock, for a while back when Cassius said

This hill is far enough,

125

there certainly was no hill. On the other hand, if you require some things to sit on it is as easy to make them look like rocks as anything else. The rock or rocks, in that case, would have to be set upon the inner stage. A further indication of its use is the mention of torches, for these would show up better in its comparative shade.

The question of costume raises difficulties. Shakespeare, by convention, dressed his Romans more or less in Elizabethan clothes. A few exotic touches may have been added. Nationality, we know, was, at times, pointed by costume. So, possibly, was period; but not, one suspects, with any consistency, not, for a certainty, with any historical accuracy. In this text, at any rate, while there are no direct indications of ' Roman habitings,' there are a round dozen of references to the Elizabethan. Therefore we cannot simply ignore Shakespeare's convention in favour of our own, which pictures the ancient Roman, bare-headed, clean shaven and wrapped in a toga.[1] But then, neither can we very easily and altogether ignore our own. The questions of costume and scenery differ in this: whatever the background, if one is kept conscious of it once the play's acting is under way, it is a bad background; but the look of the actors is of constant importance. We are in this dilemma, then. Cæsar, we hear, plucks ope his doublet; the conspirators' hats are plucked about their ears; Brutus walks unbraced and turns down the leaf of a book which he keeps in the pocket of his gown. Do these seem trivial things? Nothing

---

[1] Whether our picture is a true one is beside the point. Quite possibly the Roman Senate assembled did *not* look like the cooling-room of a Turkish bath.

in a play is trivial which bears upon the immediate credibility of the action. The theatre is a game of make-believe, and the rules of any game may be varied by use and acceptance, but mere contrariness is tiresome. An actor may point into vacancy and fill it by description, and we shall be at one with him; but to wear a toga, and call it a doublet, will be distracting. And, apart from direct verbal contradictions, there are passages enough whose full effect must remain one with the picture Shakespeare made of them. The boy Lucius asleep over his lute; who ever can have realised that episode in its exact and delicate detail and want to transform and botch it? Yet it must be confessed that a Cæsar in doublet and hose may offend and will undoubtedly distract us.

The difficulty must, I suggest, be met by compromise, in which we can find some positive advantage too. We are not concerned with the accuracy of our own picturing of Rome, but to reconcile two dramatic conventions. It goes without saying that the nearer we can in general come to Shakespeare's point of view the better. But for a particular gain, has not the vulgar modern conception of Rome, nourished on Latin lessons and the classic school of painting, become rather frigid? Are not our noble Romans, flinging their togas gracefully about them, slow-moving, consciously dignified, speaking with studied oratory and all past middle age, rather too like a schoolboy's vision of a congress of headmasters? Compare them with the high-mettled, quick-tongued crew of politicians and fighters that Shakespeare imagines; and if it comes to accuracy, has he not more the right of it than we, even though his

Cæsar be dressed in doublet and hose? So let the designer at least provide an escape from this cold classicism, which belongs neither to the true Rome nor to the play he has to interpret. His way can be the way of all compromise. What need each side insist on? The figure of Brutus must not make a modern audience think all the time of Shakespeare himself, but where the gain to Shakespeare that it should? On the other hand, whatever has been woven, even casually, into the fabric of the play, we must somehow manage to respect. If we change, we must not falsify.

The methods of the Mask and the way of Renaissance painters with classical subjects give us the hint we need. Whether from taste or lack of information, when it came to picturing Greeks and Romans they were for fancy dress; a mixture, as a rule, of helmet, cuirass, trunk hose, stockings and sandals, like nothing that ever was worn, but very wearable and delightful to look at. Women's dresses seem to have been manipulated less easily; perhaps the wearers were not so amenable, or so tolerant of the outrage upon fashion. But even here something of the sort is managed. And something of the sort, with emphasis upon this period or that, according to his judgment, will get our designer out of his difficulty. Shakespeare's own consent, so to speak, to such a compromise can be determined, for the tests are all to hand before ever the play is acted. Upon the tacit consent of an audience one can only speculate. But the problem with an audience in this as in other things is less to satisfy their opinion, if they have one, than to release them from its burden for the fuller, the un-self-

conscious, enjoyment of the play. *Julius Cæsar*!
They may come expecting the familiarised figures
set against some popular picture-book background
of Rome. For good reasons given they cannot
have this. The designer must overreach them.
He must appeal, that is to say, past expectation
and opinion, to their readiness to be pleased and
convinced; and there are no rules by which that
can be forecast. But this much law can be laid
down. He must first be sure that his work will
fuse with Shakespeare's. What Shakespeare's
purposes will not accept, he must reject. For the
rest, he may be bold or cautious as it suits him.
He had better be simple. If he can so picture
the play to himself that nothing in the picture
raises any thought but of the play, he will probably
not go far wrong.

THE MUSIC

Only one difficulty presents itself; we are given
no text for the *Music and a Song* of Act IV, Scene iii.
Custom prescribes the use of

> Orpheus with his lute made trees . . .

from *Henry VIII*, and this may well be allowed.
Mr. Richmond Noble in his *Shakespeare's Use of
Song* suggests that the stage direction in the Folio
may be a later interpolation and that no song is
called for, only the playing of an air. This he
would presumably justify by Brutus'

> Canst thou hold up thy heavy eyes awhile,
> And touch thy instrument a strain or two?

But a song would be more usual, a lute solo not
very audible in a public theatre, and the evidence

of the Folio is not negligible.[1] This apart, we have only to give careful attention to the sennets, flourishes, drums and marches, alarums, low alarums and retreats, which find place throughout the play, for they have each a particular purpose.

A STUMBLING-BLOCK IN THE TEXT

The text, as the first Folio gives it us, is an exceptionally clean one and I do not examine its few minor difficulties here. There is, however, one serious stumbling-block in Act IV. What are we to make of the duplicate revelation of Portia's death? The question has, of course, been argued high and low and round about, and weighty opinion will be found set out in the Furness *Variorum*. The weightier the worse, one is driven to complain. For surely it is clear that a mere corruption of text is involved, not the degeneracy of Brutus' character. Shakespeare may have fumbled a little at this point. But that his final intention was to give us a Brutus wantonly ' showing off ' to Messala or indulging at this moment in a super-subtle defence of his grief, I would take leave to dispute against the weightiest opinion in the world. One must, however, suggest some explanation; and here is mine. It is not provably correct, but I suggest that corrections of text are not provable. The vagaries of a

[1] Mr. Richmond Noble also says that he has recommended the use of " Weep ye no more, sad fountains," from Dowland's " Third Book of Airs." It is difficult not to recommend such an entirely beautiful song when any opportunity occurs. But the words of " Orpheus with his lute " are very appropriate; they could, indeed, be made a pertinent enough illustration of Shakespeare's use of song.

playwright's mind may be guessed at, they can never be brought within the four corners of a system and so tested.

My guess is that Shakespeare originally wrote this, or something like it:

> *Brutus.* Lucius, a bowl of wine.
> *Cassius.* I did not think you could have been so angry.[1]
>
> *Enter boy with wine, and tapers.*
>
> *Brutus.* In this I bury all unkindness, Cassius . . .

And so on as the text now stands, omitting, however, both

> *Cassius.* Portia, art thou gone?
> *Brutus.* No more, I pray you,

and (possibly)

> *Cassius.* Cicero one?
> *Messala.* Cicero is dead, and by that order of proscription.

These have something the air of additions, designed to keep Cassius active in the scene; and the first, of course, involves his knowledge of Portia's death. By this text Brutus first hears the news from Messala, and he exhibits a correct stoicism.[2] Then Shakespeare found that this made his hero not so much stoical as wooden, so he threw the disclosure back into closer conjunction with the quarrel and made it an immediate sequel to the eccentric-comic interruption by the poet. The passage here has all the air of a thing done at a breath, and by a man who had taken a fresh breath

---

[1] This line of Cassius might be a later addition.
[2] Cassius' " I have as much of this in art as you " does not tell against this, for ' art ' does not of course mean anything like ' artfulness.'

10

for it too. Whether or no thereafter he cut Messala's disclosure I do not feel positive. He may have thought there was now a double effect to be gained (the original one had not been perhaps so bad, it had only not been good enough); and, in performance, there is an arbitrary sort of effect in the passage as it stands. It is quite likely that, patching at the thing, he did not see to what subtle reflections upon Brutus' character the new combination would give rise (so seldom apparently did he consider the troubles of his future editors!). I hope that he made the cut. I think on the whole that he did. I am sure that he should have done; and I recommend the producer of to-day to make it, and by no means to involve his Brutus in that incidental lie, nor his character in the even more objectionable subtleties of an escape from it.

KING LEAR

SCHOLARS, in the past, have been apt to forbid this play the theatre; it is my business now to justify its place there. Shakespeare meant it to be acted, one might plead. Acted it undoubtedly was in his time, and seemingly with success, for his company took it to play at Whitehall before the King. Does not this settle the question? But no less a voice than Charles Lamb's is heard: Lear is essentially impossible to be represented on the stage. And, something like a century later, Dr. A. C. Bradley, though he qualifies his judgment, concludes that it is " too huge for the stage." It may be, then, that Shakespeare, " fairly caught in the web of his own imagination " (to quote Hazlitt for a third objector, as he quotes Lamb with approval), broke all bounds, and wrote the play, shall we say, for some perfect theatre laid up for him in heaven. It is not likely, we may admit, that, his mind aflame with the writing of this play or another, he stopped to measure scene after scene to the chances of a perfect performance here on earth. Such consideration makes for competent craftsmanship, no more. The greater a play the less likelihood of its perfect performing; yet, strangely enough, the less need for it. But he certainly meant this play to be acted, as acted it was; and it may be that, if we fling ourselves at the task, as Burbage and the rest had to do when he brought them a new manuscript, with something of the faith they must have had in him as a play-wright, for all his disturbing genius—it may be we shall not do so badly. But to this faith must be added something which the company from the Globe had also gained, a knowledge of his play-wright's craft.

THE NATURE OF THE PLAY

It is here that the scholars' case against the play as a play for the theatre is weak. Lamb's denunciation, indeed, was occasioned not by Shakespeare's play at all, but by Tate's perversion of it. And though he may declare that neither will he have Shakespeare's *King Lear* in the theatre, it is from nothing like Shakespeare's theatre that he bans it. Lamb's was the stage of spectacle; he bases his arguments upon it, not upon Shakespeare's. And if it was not yet the stage of hypnotic visual illusion to which the late nineteenth century accustomed us (also to be remembered when the nineteenth-century scholar is dogmatising), it had parted far enough from the stage upon which the speaker and his spoken word were all but the sole power —an audience, in the true sense, being what they swayed—from the theatre in which a blind man lost little. Visual illusion, and realism so called (though this is but the absorbing of one convention in another) have tended to make the technique of the spoken word, of rhetoric and poetry, absurd; they have shamed it to death. Lamb's theatre had not quite brought Shakespeare to this. Yet rhetoric by his time had mostly become mere rhetoric, and the great passages arbitrary occasion for vocal and emotional display. It was the age of

" the beauties of Shakespeare." That, its beauty beside, this dynamic verse and prose held secrets of stagecraft does not seem to have been considered. How indeed, with Shakespeare's stage hardly a memory, should care for its craft survive? As witness of Lamb's theatre's oblivion to it the current treatment of the text is enough; and contemporary criticism of the abuse is less of the damage done to Shakespeare than of the embellishments by which the damage is covered. The playwright was all but forgotten in the dramatic poet. And, despite our recapture of some sense of the seventeenth-century theatre and our restoration of texts, we still are disposed to think we can appreciate the plays, all appreciation of their craftsmanship apart. But Shakespeare built his castles upon a firm, familiar stage, not in the air.

We need not claim for him impeccability as a playwright. His work abounds in improvisations of technique; he is skilful, and never more skilful than when he is in a difficulty, though often enough even then it is the vitality behind the skill which pulls him through. As to rhetoric, he is capable on occasion of the wantonest use of it, and of a little fine sound and fury purely for its own sake. But when he sets himself such a task as *King Lear*, when, his imagination kindling, the full scope of such a theme opens out to him, we may expect him to be at his best—why not?—as craftsman and poet too, and to find him rallying every resource of craftsmanship to his help. For the hugeness of *Lear* these resources may still have been too few, they may have failed him at need. But of this we can be sure; it will be a case of failure, not avoidance, for his admitted task was to make his play stageworthy. In his greatest drama we should at least look for his greatest stagecraft, nor have we a right to pronounce its failure without the fullest understanding, without making the completest test of it. Further, the test must be made in the strict terms of *his* stagecraft; in no other need we expect success.

Bradley's objections to the play's staging are more carefully considered than Lamb's (which were indeed a part of a rather childish outburst against the idolatry of actors and acting in general), and they are pretty comprehensive. He holds that while " it has scenes immensely effective in the theatre "—and he quotes Lear's scene with Goneril, the later scene with her and with Regan and the reconciliation with Cordelia,—yet that " the immense scope of the work, the mass and variety of intense experience which it contains . . . the half-realised suggestions of vast universal powers working in the world of individual fates and passions—all this interferes with dramatic clearness even when the play is read, and in the theatre not only refuses to reveal itself fully through the senses but seems to be almost in contradiction with their reports." This objection as a whole involves, I fancy, a fallacy about the theatre in general, and the extreme sensibility shown in the last phrase gives us, perhaps, a clue to it. Dr. Bradley seems to assume that every sort of play, when acted, ought in a single performance to make a clear, complete and final effect on the spectator. But this is surely not so. We need no more expect to receive—lapses of performance and attention apart—the full value of a great drama at a first hearing than we expect

136

it of a complex piece of music. And what preliminary study of the music, with its straiter laws
and more homogeneous material, will effect, study
of drama will not. A play's interpretation is an
unrulier business, and we must face it rather as
we face life itself. When we gather up in our
minds the total effect made upon us by some past
personal experience, we find it to consist of the then
immediate emotion, which we can emotionally
recall, of our later judgment of the whole matter,
and—lodged between these two—of much hybrid
sensation and thought, variously recollected. Now,
it is the business of the dramatist, doubtless, in turning actuality to art, to clarify all this sort of thing
and bring it to terms. But if he aimed only at its
clear statement he would produce no illusion of life
at all; and this it is his art to do. Comedy does
aim at as much clarity as is consistent with character
kept in action. Greek tragedy blends thought and
emotion very equably; and, with music to help,
keeps the power, but keeps the constraint too, of
ritual. Does it follow, however, that Shakespeare's
method in *King Lear* is not a method like any other,
if he sets out—as I suggest he does—to provoke in us,
as we listen and look, the very confusion of feeling
and chaos of mind which will best bring us into
immediate sympathy with the play's happenings,
while, every now and then, he lodges thoughts
with us (what play is fuller of memorable phrases?)
which, with the story told, will remain for a
memory when the emotion has subsided? Why
should not the ultimate effect of this be coherent
and balanced enough? There may well be even
more meaning in *King Lear* than will come to us
thus; matter we may pick out of the text, speculate

and argue over; as, no doubt, much stayed still un-expressed in Shakespeare's own mind when he had done writing. But, again, a work of art must aim first at producing its immediate effect. And this (it is true of great art, if a negligible truth of all other) will be made a little differently upon each of us, and for each of us may differ from time to time. Abundance of power, then, there must be, and a certain waste must be allowed for. *King Lear* does perhaps over-abound in sheer power, and will be apt to excite and confuse our emotions unduly. But the corrective of thought is strongly and currently applied. And I believe we may abandon ourselves to the emotions raised by a performance, confident that the com-plete and final effect produced on us will be fruitful and equable enough, and that, though we may lose at the time in fullness of understanding, we shall gain in conviction.

The error—as I am bold enough to think it— of Dr. Bradley's contention springs possibly from a too sophisticated approach to the play. I should be surprised to hear that he first made acquaintance with it in the theatre, as Shakespeare would have had him do. Whether or no, he seems to have grown so concerned with its meta-physics that its ' physics ' have become repellent to him, and their effect, as he says, contradictory. But this is a paradox, and æsthetically not a very wholesome one. It illustrates the danger that besets all scholastic study of such an abundantly, even crudely, vital art as the art of the theatre must be. There is great delight, there is much profit in such study; but it is, in a sense, a study of causes rather than effects, not a study of the work of art itself. This, when all is said, must still be given its chance. *King Lear* was meant to be acted. Inadequate and misdirected acting of it there may be, by which we must not judge it; and no perfect performance of any play by imperfect human beings can there ever be. Shakespeare may have been wrong to make a play of it. Nor, if he did strain his medium of expression beyond endurance, would he be the first great artist to do so. But he put his purpose to the proof; and so should we—to every proof, before we ignore this for the sake of disparate gains beyond.

Lamb rests his condemnation of the play's acting upon the third act and the scenes in the storm. The passage is always being quoted. " So to see Lear acted—to see an old man tottering about the stage with a walking-stick, turned out of doors by his daughters on a rainy night— has nothing in it but what is painful and disgusting. . . . But the Lear of Shakespeare cannot be acted. The contemptible machinery by which they mimic the storm which he goes out in, is not more inadequate to represent the horrors of the real elements than any actor can be to represent Lear. . . . The greatness of Lear is not in corporal dimension, but in intellectual. . . . On the stage we see nothing but corporal infirmities and weakness, the impotence of rage; while we read it, we see not Lear but we are Lear. . . ."

Lamb states the case, let us admit, about as simply and as well as it can be stated, and he fixes upon the supreme moments of dramatic achievement and theatrical difficulty. If we meet the challenge here and make good answer, may not the rest of the play claim a verdict too? Well, Lamb's case, as I suggest, is a bad case because it shows no recognition at all of Elizabethan stagecraft; his case, in fact, is not against Shakespeare the playwright, but against his betrayal.

It is very hard to shake free from the conventions of an accustomed theatre; with the first play we see we accept them, and thereafter seldom even consider what they are. We are only conscious of offence against them; they are as a treaty we have made, upon the basis of which we surrender our imagination. We have a right to their observance, we feel. Incidentally, whenever this treaty is broken, the actors—who stand in some danger, so to speak, between the parties to it—will tend always to minimise the offence. Now there are plays, and passages of any play, in which convention may seem negligible. One could pick scenes from Shakespeare, from Euripides, from Ibsen that can be made to suit any stage and almost any sort of acting. But when a dramatist has set himself a task to tax all his resources we may look for him to fortify himself within his theatre's strongest convention. So it is, at any rate, with this third act of *King Lear*. The chief strength of Elizabethan stagecraft lay in its comprehensive use of poetry. Plot was carried on, character developed and environment created, by the aid of poetry, emotion was sustained by it and illusion held. And Shakespeare can achieve the multiple task with an abundance of skill, and conceal the achievement in beauty, often (and the better) in an amazing simplicity too. Now no such crisis as this third act presents could be compassed and wrought out in any theatre, surely, without its every technical resource being called in aid. We might look, then, to find this centre of the play a very epitome of Shakespeare's stagecraft—and we do.[1]

What is his exact dramatic need here, and how does he turn to its account this comprehensive use of verse? Be it verse or prose, he has no other resource, we must remember, than the spoken word of the actor, such action as will not mar it, and a negative background to this action. He has no accessories worth mentioning. The shaking of a thunder sheet cannot be said to count for emotional effect. It is little more than symbolic, strikes on the emotions hardly more than do the ' alarums ' and ' retreats ' which mark the progress of a battle, and less, probably, than the sounding of a trumpet or a ' drum far off.' Music he might command, it is true, but none that could help him to the raising of this storm. Lear, Kent and the rest must *act* the storm then ; there is no other way. They must not lose themselves in its description; it will not do for us to be interested in the storm at the expense of our

---

[1] Incidentally, we may do best, as students, to approach *King Lear*, not even through the Folio—though this spares us all the editorial accretions of the pictorial stage—but through the yet greater simplicity, the very crudity of the Quartos, which record neither acts nor scenes and often leave us guessing whether characters are on the stage or off. For this will be a sharp corrective to our instinctive lodging of the play among the diversities and distractions of a modern theatre. Diversity, of course, will appear when the play is acted and each character moves integrally before us. The unity of the whole in a reader's imagination will be replaced by the unruliness and imperfections which belong to this; but by its human actuality, too, which is imagination's safe anchor. This diversity asserted, the art of production is to bring it again to a unity of effect.

interest in them, the loss there would be more than the gain. For the effect of the storm upon Lear is Shakespeare's true objective. So he has to give it magnitude without detracting for one precious moment during the crisis from Lear's own dramatic supremacy. And he solves his problem by making the actor impersonate Lear and the storm together, by identifying Lear's passion with the storm's. Mere association will not serve; there must be no chance left of a rivalry of interest. For that again might set the sensations of the audience at odds and dissipate the play's power upon them. This puts the thing crudely, and Shakespeare's skill in enriching and masking his main effect with minor ones (lest we grow too conscious of what he is doing and resist him) is amazing. But this is the basis of his stage-craft, to make Lear and the storm as one. And if Lamb saw " an old man tottering about the stage with a walking-stick " he did not see the Lear of Shakespeare's intention.

> Blow winds, and crack your cheeks! rage! blow!
> You cataracts and hurricanoes, spout
> Till you have drench'd our steeples, drown'd the cocks!
> You sulphurous and thought-executing fires,
> Vaunt-couriers to oak-cleaving thunderbolts,
> Singe my white head! And thou, all-shaking thunder,
> Strike flat the thick rotundity o' the world!
> Crack nature's moulds, all germens spill at once,
> That make ingrateful man!

This is the storm itself in its tragic purpose, as Shakespeare's imagination gives it voice. And any actor who should try to speak the lines realistically in the character of a feeble old man would be a fool. There is no realism about it.

No real man could or would talk so. But the convention enables Shakespeare to isolate Lear for the time from all pettier circumstance, to symbolise the storm in him, and so to make him the great figure which the greater issues of the play demand.[1] The actor must make both himself, and, for the moment, the lesser Lear—the Lear of infirmities and humours—forgotten as he speaks the lines; not such a hard thing to do if, without forgetting he is Lear, he yet speaks them for their own sake, for they outpace humanity. The lesser Lear will be recalled to us—and with interest—when Shakespeare wants him to be.

To heighten even this heroic height by contrast, we have next the shrill, pitiful chatter of the Fool:

O nuncle, court holy-water in a dry house is better than this rain-water out o' door. Good nuncle, in, ask thy daughters' blessing; here's a night pities neither wise men nor fools.

Then, again, the Promethean Lear:

Rumble thy bellyfull! Spit, fire! spout, rain!
Nor rain, wind, thunder, fire, are my daughters:
I tax not you, you elements, with unkindness;
I never gave you kingdom, call'd you children,
You owe me no subscription: then let fall
Your horrible pleasure; here I stand, your slave,
A poor, infirm, weak, and despis'd old man.

Does it matter that, compassing the grandeur of the defiance, he will not seem of a sudden, as he

---

[1] He sets up a signpost for actor and audience both. The King, Kent is told a little earlier,

Contending with the fretful elements . . .
Strives in his little world of man to outscorn
The to-and-fro conflicting wind and rain.

says it, either poor, infirm, or weak? Not one bit. Shakespeare gains the effect he needs here by the meaning of the words and the change in their music, by the quick shift from magniloquence to a line of perfect simplicity. There, by virtue of that effect, stands the man Lear restored to us again, and with interest; pathetic by contrast with these elements, yet still terribly great by his identity with our sense of them. And this is the Lear, great not in corporal but in intellectual dimensions, the Lear of Lamb's demand.

THE MAIN LINES OF CONSTRUCTION

King Lear, alone among the great tragedies, adds to its plot a sub-plot fully developed. And it suffers under the burden. After a few preliminary lines—Shakespeare had come to prefer this to the grand opening, and in this instance they are made introductory to plot and sub-plot too—we have a full and almost formal statement of the play's main theme and a show of the characters that are to develop it, followed by a scene which sets out the sub-plot as fully. The two scenes together form a sort of double dramatic prologue; and they might, by modern custom, count as a first act, for after them falls the only clearly indicated time-division in the play. The Folio, however, adds the quarrel with Goneril before an act-pause is allowed: then—whatever its authority, but according to its usual plan—sets out four more acts, the second allotted to the parallel quarrel with Regan, the third to the climax of the main theme; the fourth we may call a picture of the wreck of both Lear and

Gloucester, and in it sub-plot and main plot are blended, and the fifth act is given to the final and rather complex catastrophe. This division, then, has thus much dramatic validity, and a producer may legitimately choose to abide by it. On the other hand, one may contend, the play's action flows unchecked throughout (but for the one check which does not coincide with the act-division of the Folio). Still it is not to be supposed that a Jacobean audience did, or a modern audience would, sit through a performance without pause. Yet again, it does not follow that the Folio's act-divisions were observed as intervals in which the audience dispersed and by which the continuity of dramatic effect was altogether broken. A producer must, I think, exercise his own judgment. There may be something to be said for more 'breathing spaces,' but I should myself incline to one definite interval only, to fall after Act III. To this point the play is carried by one great impetus of inspiration, and there will be great gain in its acting being as unchecked. If the strain on actors or audience seems to be too great, I should choose a breathing space after Act I, Scene ii, for all the Folio's authority to the contrary. But the strain should not be excessive upon either audience or actors. Shakespeare's stagecraft—his interweaving of contrasted characters and scenes—provides against this, as does the unity of impression and rapidity of action, which his unlocalised staging makes possible.[1]

---

[1] Modern scenic productions, even at their simplest, not only destroy this unity of impression, but lengthen the performance of the plays considerably, and the acting habits they have engendered lengthen them still more. Mr. Nugent

The scene in which Lear divides his kingdom is a magnificent statement of a magnificent theme. It has a proper formality, and there is a certain megalithic grandeur about it, Lear dominating it, that we associate with Greek tragedy. Its probabilities are neither here nor there. A dramatist may postulate any situation he has the means to interpret, if he will abide by the logic of it after. The producer should observe and even see stressed the scene's characteristics; Lear's two or three passages of such an eloquence as we rather expect at a play's climax than its opening, the strength of such single lines as

The bow is bent and drawn, make from the shaft,

with its hammering monosyllables; and the hard-bitten

Nothing: I have sworn; I am firm,

together with the loosening of the tension in changes to rhymed couplets, and the final drop into prose by that business-like couple, Goneril and Regan. Then follows, with a lift into lively verse for a start, as a contrast and as the right medium for Edmund's sanguine conceit, the development of the Gloucester theme. Shakespeare does this at his ease, allows himself diversion and time. He has now both the plot of the ungrateful daughters and the sub-plot of the treacherous son under way.

Monck has produced *King Lear* at the Maddermarket Theatre, Norwich, upon an unlocalised stage. He cut approximately 750 of the 3340 lines of text (the Folio will give authority for the cutting of some 200), allowed a ten minutes' interval, did not play over-rapidly, and the whole performance only lasted two hours and a half.

But the phenomenon for which Shakespeareans learn to look has not yet occurred, that inexplicable 'springing to life'—a springing, it almost seems, into a life of its own—of character or theme. Very soon it does occur; Lear's entrance, disburdened from the care of state, is its natural signal. On his throne, rightly enough, he showed formal and self-contained. Now he springs away; and now the whole play in its relation to him takes on a liveliness and variety; nor is the energy to be checked or weakened, or, if checked, only that the next stroke may be intenser, till the climax is past, till his riven and exhausted nature is granted the oblivion of sleep. This is the master-movement of the play, which enshrines the very soul of the play—and in the acting, as I have suggested, there should be no break allowed. To read and give full imaginative value to those fifteen hundred lines at a stretch is certainly exhausting; if they were written at one stretch of inspiration the marvel is that Shakespeare, with his Lear, did not collapse under the strain, yet the exactions of its performance he tempers with all his skill. Lear is surrounded by characters, which each in a different way take a share of the burden from him. Kent, the Fool, and Edgar as Poor Tom are a complement of dramatic strength; and the interweaving of the scenes concerning Oswald, Edmund and Gloucester saves the actor's energy for the scenes of the rejection and the storm.[1]

---

[1] Therefore the producer who will for the sake of his scenery (as has been the pleasant picture-stage custom) run two or three of the storm scenes into one, presents himself and his Lear with failure.

As the Lear theme expanded under his hand Shakespeare had begun, and perforce, to economise his treatment of the Gloucester–Edgar–Edmund story. Edgar himself is indeed dismissed from the second scene upon no more allowance of speech than

> I'm sure on't, not a word

—with which the best of actors may find it hard to make his presence felt; and at our one view of him before he had been left negative enough. Edmund is then brought rapidly into relation with the main plot, and the blending of main plot and sub-plot begins.[1] Edgar also is drawn into

---

[1] We find, too, at this point, some signs that the emphasis of the play's whole scheme was altered.

> Have you heard of no likely wars toward
> 'Twixt the Dukes of Cornwall and Albany?

Curan asks Edmund, who answers "Not a word." Edmund, with admirable promptitude, turns the notion to the further confusing of the so easily confused Edgar, but the wars themselves come to nothing. Kent, in an involved speech in Act III (for him most uncharacteristically involved), suggests that it is the threat of them which is bringing the French army to England. But the vagueness is suspicious. It looks a little as if Shakespeare had thought of making the hypocrite inheritors of Cordelia's portion fall out over it (an obvious nemesis) and had changed his mind. There are slight signs indeed that greed of possessions was to have been the axis for the whole play to turn upon. It begins with the parting of the realm; and

> Legitimate Edgar, I must have your land

is the coping point of Edmund's first soliloquy. Did the discovery of deeper spiritual issues in Lear's own character and fate give us the present play? Another and a later change in the plot can be divined. The King of France comes armed with Cordelia to Lear's rescue, as is natural. Then, by virtue of the clumsiest few lines in the play, he is sent back again. Did Shakespeare originally mean Cordelia

Lear's orbit; and, for the time, to the complete sacrifice of his own interests in the play. 'Poor Tom' is in effect an embodiment of Lear's frenzy, the disguise no part of Edgar's own development.

As we have seen, while Act III is at the height of its argument, Shakespeare is careful to keep alive the lower-pitched theme of Edmund's treachery, his new turn to the betrayal of his father. He affords it two scenes, of twenty-five lines each, wedged between the three dominant scenes of the storm and Lear's refuge from it.

---

to restore her father to his throne as in the old play; but would a French victory in England not have done? It may be; though I cannot think he ever intended Lear to survive. On the other hand, Cordelia herself is not a figure predoomed to death. This catastrophe, though the moral violence of the play may æsthetically justify it, and though it is needed dramatically, as a final blow to Lear (see p. 182 for the fuller argument of this), always seems to me a wrench from his first plan. This decided on though, he would certainly have to get rid of France. The point for the producer is that the Folio cuts the clumsy explanation, as if on the principle—and it is an excellent one in the theatre—of: " Never explain, never apologise." In fact it cuts the whole scene, which later contains as dramatically feeble an excuse for the delay in handing Lear over to his daughter's care, though it gives none for the devoted Kent letting the distracted old man out of his sight to roam the fields crowned with wild flowers. I think on the whole that the Folio gives a producer a good lead. Yet another slight change of plan may be guessed at; it would effect some economy in the working out of the sub-plot. Edmund says to Gloucester about Edgar:

If your honour judge it meet, I will place you where you shall hear us confer of this . . . and that without any further delay than this very evening.

But he never does. Shakespeare may have remembered, besides, that he had lately used this none too fresh device in *Othello*.

They are sufficient and no more for their own purpose; in their sordidness they stand as valuable contrast to the spiritual exaltation of the others. The supreme moment for Lear himself, the turning-point, therefore, of the play's main theme, is reached in the second of the three storm scenes, when the proud old king kneels humbly and alone in his wretchedness to pray. This is the argument's absolute height; and from now on we may feel (as far as Lear is concerned) the tension relax, through the first grim passage of his madness, slackening still through the fantastic scene of the arraignment of the joint-stools before that queer bench of justices, to the moment of his falling asleep and his conveyance away—his conveyance, we find it to be, out of the main stream of the play's action. Shakespeare then deals the dreadful blow to Gloucester. The very violence and horror of this finds its dramatic justification in the need to match in another sort—since he could not hope to match it in spiritual intensity—the catastrophe to Lear. And now we may imagine him, if we please, stopping to consider where he was. Anti-climax, after this, is all but inevitable. Let the producer take careful note how Shakespeare sets out to avoid the worst dangers of it.[1]

---

[1] It is worth remarking here upon the fact that of Edgar's two soliloquies—the one which ends Act III, Scene vi, and the one which begins Act IV—the Folio omits the first. They are somewhat redundant in mood if not in matter. The interesting thing is that the Folio omission is of a speech ending a scene and moralising upon the event; it forms a 'considering point.' Without it the catastrophe to Gloucester is linked more closely to Lear's misfortunes, and the long due development of Edgar's character then begins—and

Had the play been written upon the single subject of Lear and his daughters, we should now be in sight of its end. But the wealth of material Shakespeare has posited asks for use, and his own imagination, we may suppose, is still teeming. But by the very nature of the material (save Cordelia) left for development the rest of the play must be pitched in a lower key. Shakespeare marshals the action by which the wheel of Gloucester's weakness and Edmund's treachery is brought full circle with extraordinary skill and even more extraordinary economy. Yet for all this, except in a fine flash or two, the thing stays by comparison pedestrian. He is only on the wing again when Lear and Cordelia are his concern; in the scenes of their reconciliation and of the detached tragedy of Lear's death with the dead Cordelia in his arms, as in the still more detached and—as far as the mere march of the action is concerned—wholly unjustifiable scene of Lear mad and fantastically crowned with wild flowers. We must add, though, to the inspired passages the immediately preceding fantasy of Gloucester's imaginary suicide, a cunning set-off to the actual horror of his blinding, and occasion for some inimitable verse. The chief fact to face, then, is that for the rest of the play, the best will be incidental and not germane to the actual story.[1] The producer therefore must give his

importantly—the fourth Act. For further argument upon this point, see pp. 211, 227.

[1] The meeting of mad Lear and blind Gloucester (I give the scene more attention on p. 179) is, of course, most germane to the play's *idea*—a more important thing to Shakespeare than the mere story—but it does check the march of the story.

own best attention to Albany, Goneril, and Regan and their close-packed contests, and to the nice means by which Edgar is shaped into a hero; and in general must see that this purposeful disciplined necessary stuff is given fullness and, as far as may be, spontaneity of life in its interpretation. If he will take care of this the marvellous moments will tend to take care of him.

Shakespeare strengthens the action at once with the fresh interest of the Edmund–Goneril–Regan intrigue, daring as it is to launch into this with the short time left him for its development and resolving. He is, indeed, driven to heroic compressions, to implications, effects by ' business,' action ' off,' almost to ' love-making by reference only.' Goneril's first approach to Edmund (or his to her; but we may credit the lady, I think, with the throwing of the handkerchief) is only clearly marked out for the actors by Regan's reference to it five scenes later, when she tells us that at Goneril's

> . . . late being here
> She gave strange œilliads and most speaking looks
> To noble Edmund.

(Regan credits her with what, if we prefer our Shakespeare modernized, we might literally translate into ' giving the glad eye.') But this silent business of the earlier scene is important and must be duly marked if the arrival of the two together and Edmund's turning back to avoid meeting Albany, the ' mild husband,' is to have its full effect. For the first and last of their spoken love-making, excellently characteristic as it is, consists of Goneril's

152

Our wishes on the way
May prove effects. . . .
This trusty servant
Shall pass between us: ere long you are like to hear,
If you dare venture in your own behalf,
A mistress's command. Wear this; spare speech;
Decline your head: this kiss, if it durst speak,
Would stretch thy spirits up into the air.
Conceive, and fare thee well.

and Edmund's (" Spare speech," indeed!)

Yours in the ranks of death!

—all spoken in Oswald's presence, too. It is, of course, not only excellent but sufficient. The regal impudency of the woman, the falsely chivalrous flourish of the man's response—pages of dialogue might not tell us more of their relations; and, of such relations, is there much more that is dramatically worth knowing? The point for the producer is that no jot of such a constricted dramatic opportunity must be missed.

For the whole working out of this lower issue of the play the same warning stands true; an exact and unblurred value must be given to each significant thing. The interaction of circumstance and character is close-knit and complex, but it is clear. Keep it clear and it can be made effective to any audience that will listen, and is not distracted from listening. Let us underline this last phrase and now make the warning two-fold. In working out a theme so full of incident and of contending characters Shakespeare allows for no distraction of attention at all, certainly not for the breaking of continuity which the constant shifting of realistically localised scenery must involve. The action, moreover, of these later scenes is exceptionally dependent upon to-ings and fro-ings. Given continuity of performance and no more insistence upon whereabouts than the action itself will indicate, the impression produced by the constant busy movement into our sight and out again of purposeful, passionate or distracted figures, is in itself of great dramatic value, and most congruous to the plot and counter-plot of the play's ending. The order for Lear's and Cordelia's murder, the quarrel over Edmund's precedence, Albany's sudden self-assertion, Regan's sickness, Edgar's appearance, the fight, his discovery of himself, Goneril's discomfiture, the telling of Kent's secret, Regan's and Goneril's death, the alarm to save Lear and Cordelia—Shakespeare, by the Folio text, gets all this into less than two hundred lines, with a fair amount of rhetoric and incidental narrative besides. He needs no more, though bareness does nearly turn to banality sometimes. But unless we can be held in an unrelaxed grip we may not submit to the spell.

He has kept a technical master-stroke for his ending:

Enter Lear with Cordelia in his arms.

There should be a long, still pause, while Lear passes slowly in with his burden, while they all stand respectful as of old to his majesty. We may have wondered a little that Shakespeare should be content to let Cordelia pass from the play as casually as she seems to in the earlier scene. But this is the last of her, not that. Dumb and dead, she that was never apt of speech—what fitter finish for her could there be? What fitter ending to the history of the two of them, which

began for us with Lear on his throne, conscious
of all eyes on him, while she shamed and angered
him by her silence? The same company are
here, or all but the same, and they await his
pleasure.[1] Even Regan and Goneril are here to
pay him a ghastly homage. But he knows none
of them—save for a blurred moment Kent whom
he banished—none but Cordelia. And again he
reproaches her silence; for

> Her voice was ever soft,
> Gentle and low, an excellent thing in woman.

Then his heart breaks.

THE METHOD OF THE DIALOGUE

The dialogue of *King Lear* is remarkable for its
combination of freedom and power. Of the plays
that neighbour it, the sustained use of verse in
Othello may make for greater unity and nobility
of effect. In *Macbeth* there are passages that
seem to wield a sort of secret sway. *Antony and
Cleopatra* has ease and breadth for its normal
virtues as *Coriolanus* has strength; and, after,
Shakespeare passes to his last period of varied
and delightful ease. But the exact combination
of qualities that distinguishes the writing of *King
Lear* we do not find again; nor indeed should we
look to, for it is the product of the matter and
the nature of the play. Shakespeare was in

[1] And this must not be counted as chance, for the bodies
of Goneril and Regan are brought on—why else?—and
the dying Edmund, who might as well be dead and no
great inconvenience, is removed. (He may have been a
spectator of the earlier scene, but a quite unregarded
spectator.)

nothing a finer artist than in this, that, once he
had mastered his means of expression, having
journeyed from the rhymed couplets and fantastic
prose of *Love's Labour's Lost* to the perfected verse
and balanced prose of *Henry V* and the mature
comedies, he yet fettered himself in no fixed style.
He may write carelessly; here and there in his
greatest scenes we find couplets of cynical bombast
and lines flatter than a pancake.[1] But, his
imagination once fired, the idea seldom fails of
the very living vesture it needs. This, it may be
said, it is any writer's business to discover. But
Shakespeare's art lies in the resource, which can
give individual expression to a thought or emotion
within the bounds, for instance, of a stretch of
formal verse if his first need is for the solid strength
of this; or, more often, in the moulding of verse
and prose into such variety of expressive form
that it is a wonder any unity of effect is kept at
all—yet it is. It lies in the daring by which, for
a scene or two, he may dispense with all unity of
form whatever, if his dramatic purpose will so
profit. Witness such a seemingly haphazard mixture of verse, prose and snatches of song as we
find in the scenes between Lear, Kent, Gloucester,
the Fool and Poor Tom. Yet the dramatic
vitality of these scenes lies largely in this variety

---

[1] Edmund may be dying, but surely Shakespeare might
rouse him, if he would, to something livelier than

> This speech of yours hath mov'd me
> And shall, perchance, do good, but speak you on;
> You look as you had something more to say.

I challenge any actor to give colour to that last line. Still,
as a rule, bombast or flatness, this incorrigible man of the
theatre knew when the occasion would carry a thing off.

and balance of orchestration; their emotional strain might be intolerable without it. But the root of the matter, of course, is in the imaginative vitality with which he dowers the characters themselves. It is always instructive to watch Shakespeare getting his play with its crew under way, to see him stating his subject, setting his characters in opposition. Some lead off, fully themselves from the start, some seem to hang on his hands, saying what they have to say in sound conventional phrase, some he may leave all but mute, uncertain yet, it would seem, of his own use for them. Not till the whole organism has gathered strength and abounds in a life of its own is the true mastery to be seen. Even so, in *King Lear* there is more to be accounted for. In no other of the plays, I think, unless it be *Macbeth*, are we so conscious of the force of an emotion over-riding, often, a character's self-expression, and of a vision of things to which the action itself is but a foreground. And how this and the rest of the play's individuality is made manifest by the form as well as the substance of the dialogue, by the shaping and colour of its verse and prose, it is, of course, of primary importance for producer and actors to observe. There is no one correct way of speaking Shakespeare's verse and prose, for he had no one way of writing it. One way grew out of another with him. Little of the method of *Romeo and Juliet* will be left in *King Lear*, much of the method of *Hamlet* still may be. But the fresh matter of a play will provoke a fresh manner, and its interpretation must be as freshly approached.

For more reasons and in more directions than

KING LEAR

one, Shakespeare seeks strength in simplicity in
the writing of *King Lear*. The noble conventional
speech of its beginning will not serve him long,
for this is the language of such an authority as Lear
discards. There is needed an expression of those
fiercer, cruder strengths which come into play when
a reign of order ends and a moral code is broken.
Edmund begins glibly, but is indulged neither
with subtle thought nor fine phrases. Goneril
becomes like a woman with a fever in her: " I'll
not endure it . . . I will not speak with him . . .
the fault of it I'll answer . . . I'd have it come
to question . . . I would breed from hence
occasions, and I shall. . . ." Mark how broken
is the eloquence of Lear's appeal to Regan;
mark the distraction of his

> No, you unnatural hags,
> I will have such revenges on you both
> That all the world shall—I will do such things,
> What they are yet I know not, but they shall be
> The terrors of the earth. You think I'll weep;
> No, I'll not weep:
> I have full cause of weeping, but this heart
> Shall break into a hundred thousand flaws
> Or ere I'll weep.

Here, one would say, is verse reduced to its very
elements.

Shakespeare has, besides, to carry us into
strange regions of thought and passion, so he
must, at the same time, hold us by familiar things.
Lear, betrayed and helpless, at an end of his
command of self or circumstance, is dramatically
set above the tyranny and logic of both by being
made one with the storm, and by his harmonizing
with the homely fantasies of the Fool and the mad
talk of Poor Tom, till his own 'noble anger'

breaks the bounds of reason too. Without some anchorage in simplicity, this action and these characters would so range that human interpretation could hardly compass them. Kent does something to keep the play's feet firm on the ground, Gloucester a little, the Fool was to Shakespeare's audience a familiar and sympathetic figure. But Lear himself might escape our closer sympathy were it not for his recurrent coming down from the heights to such moments as

> No, I will be the pattern of all patience;
> I will say nothing;

as

> My wits begin to turn.
> Come on, my boy. How dost, my boy? Art cold?
> I am cold myself. Where is this straw, my fellow?

as

> No, I will weep no more. In such a night
> To shut me out! Pour on, I will endure.
> In such a night as this!

or as

> Make no noise, make no noise; draw the curtains; so, so, so.
> We'll go to supper i' the morning; so, so, so.

This final stroke, moreover, brings us to the simplest physical actualities; Lear's defiance of the elements has flickered down to a mock pulling of the curtains round his bed. Later, when he wanders witless and alone, his speech is broken into oracular fragments of rhapsody; but the play of thought is upon actuality and his hands are at play all the time with actual things; with the flower (is it?) he takes for a coin, with whatever serves for a bit of cheese, for his gauntlet, his hat, for the challenge thrust under Gloucester's blind eyes.

Let us note, too, how one of the finest passages of poetry in the play, Edgar's imaginary tale of Dover cliff, consists of the clearest cut actualities of description And when Lear wakes to his right senses again, simplicity is added to simplicity in his feeling the pin's prick, in his remembering not his garments. The tragic beauty of his end is made more beautiful by his call for a looking-glass, his catching at the feather to put on Cordelia's lips, the undoing of the button. These things are the necessary balance to the magniloquence of the play's beginning and to the tragic splendour of the storm.

Amid the sustained magnificence of the first scene we find the first use of an even more simple device, recurrent throughout the play.

> . . . what can you say to draw
> A third more opulent than your sisters? Speak.
> Nothing, my lord.
> Nothing?
> Nothing.
> Nothing will come of nothing; speak again.

Again and again with varying purpose and effect Shakespeare uses this device of reiteration. Note Edmund's

> . . . Why brand they us
> With base? with baseness? bastardy? base, base?
> . . . . . . Well, then,
> Legitimate Edgar, I must have your land.
> Our father's love is to the bastard, Edmund,
> As to the legitimate: Fine word,—legitimate!
> Well, my legitimate, if this letter speed,
> And my invention thrive, Edmund the base
> Shall top the legitimate.

The repetition itself does much to drive in on us the insistent malice of the man.

Lear summons Oswald with

> O! you sir, you sir—come you hither, sir.
> Who am I, sir?

and the tragic counterpart of this is

> Hear, Nature, hear! dear goddess, hear.

Gloucester's grieved refrain falls casually enough:

> O, madam, my old heart is crack'd, is crack'd.
> . . . O lady, lady, shame would have it hid.
> . . . I know not, madam; 'tis too bad, too bad.

And for a rounded elaboration of the effect, we have Lear's

> O, reason not the need; our basest beggars
> Are in the poorest thing superfluous:
> Allow not nature more than nature needs,
> Man's life is cheap as beast's. Thou art a lady;
> If only to go warm were gorgeous,
> Why, nature needs not what thou gorgeous wear'st
> Which scarcely keeps thee warm. But, for true need—
> You heavens, give me that patience, patience I need!

Half a dozen other such instances, more or less elaborate, of major and minor importance, can be found; till we come to the effect at its crudest in

Howl, howl, howl, howl! O, you are men of stones . . .

and to the daring and magic of

> Thou'lt come no more.
> Never, never, never, never, never.

It is a simple device indeed, but all mature artists tend to seek strength in simplicity of expression. It is, at its simplest, a very old device, and older than drama. Iteration casts, of itself, a spell upon the listener, and the very sound of that echoing ' Never ' can make us sharers in Lear's helplessness and despair.[1] Bradley says of this last speech that it leaves us " on the topmost peaks of poetry "; and so, surely, it does. Rend it from its context, the claim sounds absurd; but dramatic poetry is never to be judged apart from the action it implies.

King Lear, it is said, cannot be acted. The whole scheme and method of its writing is a contrivance for its effective acting. This contrast and reconciliation of grandeur and simplicity, this setting of vision in terms of actuality, this inarticulate passion which breaks now and again into memorable phrases—does not even the seeming failure of expression give us a sense of the helplessness of humanity pitted against higher powers? All the magnificent art of this is directed to one end; the play's acting in a theatre.

---

[1] It is, moreover, an old device with Shakespeare. Set beside Lear's

> O reason not the need . . .

Juliet's

> Hath Romeo slain himself? Say thou but ' I '
> And that bare vowel ' I ' shall poison more
> Than the death-dealing eye of cockatrice.
> I am not I, if there be such an ' I,'
> Or those eyes shut that make thee answer ' I.'
> If he be slain say ' I,' or if not, no;
> Brief sounds determine of my weal or woe.

The puns may destroy its emotional value for us, though they did not for the Elizabethans. But the effect aimed at is about the same. The difference in the means to it may be made one measure of Shakespeare's development of his art. Not but that he could pun dramatically to the end. He came, however, to prefer single shots to fusillades.

162

Lear

Lear himself is so dominant a figure that the exhaustion of his impetus to action with the play's end barely in sight leaves Shakespeare, as we have argued, a heavy task in the rallying of its forces for what is still to do. The argument has been raised by then, moreover, to such imaginative heights that any descent from them—even Lear's own—must be precarious. They are heights that Shakespeare himself, perhaps, did not clearly envisage till the soaring had begun. Not that there is anything tentative in the presentation of Lear. Never was character in play, one exclaims, so fully and immediately, so imminently and overwhelmingly set forth! But in this lies the actor's first difficulty.

By the dividing of the kingdom and Cordelia's rejection the trend of the action is clearly foreshadowed.

> So be my grave my peace, as here I give
> Her father's heart from her.

By all the rules of drama we know within a little what the retribution for that must amount to; and Shakespeare will not disappoint us. But equally it would seem that for this massive fortress of pride which calls itself Lear, for any old man indeed of eighty and upwards, there could be no dramatic course but declension. Who would ever think of developing, of expanding, a character from such overwhelming beginnings? Yet this is what Shakespeare does, and finds a transcendent way to do. So the actor's difficulty is

12   163

that he must start upon a top note, at what must
be pretty well the full physical stretch of his
powers, yet have in reserve the means to a greater
climax of another sort altogether. It is here,
however, that the almost ritual formality of the
first scene will help him. The occasion itself,
the general subservience to Lear's tyranny (Kent's
protest and Cordelia's resolution only emphasise
this), Lear's own assertion of kingship as something not far from godhead, all combine to set
him so above and apart from the rest that the
very isolation will seem strength if the actor takes
care to sustain it.[1] There need be, there must
be, no descent to petulance. Lear marking the
map with his finger might be marking the land
itself, so Olympian should he appear. The oath
by the sacred radiance of the sun is one that only
he may swear. That Kent should call him an
' old man ' is in itself a blasphemous outrage.

Come not between the dragon and his wrath. . . .
The bow is bent and drawn, make from the shaft. . . .
Nothing: I have sworn; I am firm.

Lines like these mark the level of Lear. Their
fatality may be a thought mitigated by the
human surliness of

Better thou
Had'st not been born than not to have pleased me better ;

by the grim humour which lies in

Nothing will come of nothing: speak again ;

---

[1] In Reinhardt's Berlin production of the play, he placed
Lear for this first scene upon an exaggeratedly high throne
and so suggested just this isolation. A good and most
picturesque idea; but one must not depend too much on
such symbolism.

in the ironic last fling at Kent of

> Away! By Jupiter,
> *This* shall not be revoked;

and in the bitter gibe to Burgundy :

> When she was dear to us we did hold her so,
> But now her price is fall'n ;

even, one would like to suspect, in the reason given for his fast intent to shake all cares of state from him, that he may

> Unburden'd crawl toward death.

And our next sight of his Majesty is to be back from hunting with a most impatient appetite for dinner! Note too, the hint of another Lear, given us in the music of three short words—the first touch in the play of that peculiar verbal magic Shakespeare could command—when, sated with Goneril's and Regan's flattery, he turns to his Cordelia with

> Now, our joy . . .

But Lear must leave this first scene as he entered it, more a magnificent portent than a man.

He has doffed his kingship; free from its trappings, how the native genius of the man begins to show! It flashes on us as might the last outbursts of some near-extinct volcano. He is old and uncertain; but a mighty man, never a mere tyrant divested of power. He has genius, warped and random genius though it may be, and to madness, as will appear, very near allied. And Shakespeare's art is in showing us this in nothing he does—for all that he does now is foolish—but in every trivial thing that he is. All the action of the scene of the return from hunting, all his surroundings are staged to this end. The swift exchanges with the disguised Kent and their culmination:

Dost thou know me, fellow?
No, sir, but you have that in your countenance which I would fain call master.
What's that?
Authority

—his encounter with the pernickity jack-in-office Oswald, with the frail, whimsical Fool who mockingly echoes his passionate whimsies; all this sets off and helps set in motion a new and more vivid Lear. Not that Shakespeare bates us one jot of the old man's stiff-necked perversities. He no more asks our sympathy on easy terms for him than will Lear yield an inch to Goneril's reasonable requests. A hundred useless knights about the house—even though, from their master's point of view, they were men of choice and rarest parts—must have been a burden. Lear's striking Oswald really was an outrage; after due complaint Goneril would doubtless have reproved his impertinence—for all that she had prompted it. Even with the petted Fool, and in the very midst of the petting, out there snaps

Take heed, sirrah, the whip!

We need look for no tractable virtues in him.

The play's story has its appointed way to go, but here begins the way of Lear's soul's agony and salvation as Shakespeare is to blaze it. The change shows first in the dialogue with the attendant knight and the delicate strokes which inform it. The knight, dispatched to bid that mongrel

Oswald come back, returns only to report the fellow's round answer that he would not. "He would not!" flashes Lear at the unbelievable phrase. But when, picking his words—as, if you were not a Kent (and there had been room at the best for but one Kent at Court), no doubt you learned to do with Lear—the knight hints hesitatingly at trouble, the quiet response comes:

> Thou but remember'st me of mine own conception: I have perceived a most faint neglect of late; which I have rather blamed as mine own jealous curiosity, than as a very pretence and purpose of unkindness: I will look further into 't. But where's my fool? I have not seen him this two days.
> Since my young lady's going into France, sir, the fool hath much pined away.
> No more of that; I have noted it well. Go you, and tell my daughter I would speak with her. Go you, call hither my fool. O! you sir, you sir, come you hither, sir!

—for the mongrel Oswald has appeared again. Lear—can this be the Lear of the play's first scene?—to be turning his knight's "great abatement of kindness" to "a most faint neglect," and blaming, even so, his own jealous curiosity for noting it! But the Fool's grief for Cordelia he has noted well. Lest it echo too loudly in his proud unhappy heart, with a quick turn he brings the old Lear to his rescue, rasps an order here, an order there, and—takes it out of Oswald.

From now on the picturing of him is lifelike, in that it has all the varied, unexpected, indirect and latent eloquence of life. Shakespeare is at his deftest, his medium at its freest and most supple. But the interpreter must be alert too. This Lear is as quick on the uptake as it is his

Fool's business to be. An unnatural quickness
in an old man, is it, and some sign of a toppling
brain? His silences are as pregnant. He listens
and finds cheer in the Fool's chatter and song,
throws him an answer or so to keep it alive, snarls
now and then like an old lion if a sting goes too
deep; yet his thoughts, we can tell, are away.
We must visualise this scene fully and accurately;
the Fool carolling, his poor heart being heavy with
Cordelia's loss he carols the more; the old king
brooding; and Kent ever watchful, with a dog's
eyes.[1] Mark the effect of Goneril's appearance
before her father, in purposed, sullen muteness;
the Fool's speech points it for us, should we be
unobservant; then her break into the prepared
formality of verse, as this verse will seem, capping
the loose prose of the scene and the Fool's rhyming.
Mark, too, the cold kingliness of Lear's four words,
all his response to her careful address:

> Are you our daughter?

He resorts to irony, the fine mind's weapon,
which blunts itself upon the stupid—for Goneril
is stupid, and she has stupidity's consistent strength.
But when the storm of Lear's wrath does break, I
think she inwardly shakes a little.

> You strike my people, and your disordered rabble
> Make servants of their betters,

sounds like scared bravado. She can wait, though,
for the storm to pass; and it does pass in senile
self-reproaches. A few more such futile outbursts, she is sure, and the old tyrant will be

[1] Lear asks the Fool almost fretfully, " When were you
wont to be so full of songs, sirrah? " But I fancy Lear has
no need to ask when or why.

tame enough. But, suddenly, the servants are dismissed and she is alone with husband and father. And her father, rigid, transformed, and with slow, calm, dreadful strength, is calling down the gods' worst curse upon her.

> Hear, Nature, hear! dear goddess, hear!
> Suspend thy purpose if thou didst intend
> To make this creature fruitful. . . .

The actor who will rail and rant this famous passage may know his own barnstorming business, but he is no interpreter of Shakespeare. The merely superficial effect of its deadlier quiet, lodged between two whirlwinds of Lear's fury, should be obvious. But its dramatic purpose far outpasses that. Not indifferently did Shakespeare make this a pagan play, and deprive its argument of comfortable faith in virtue rewarded, here or hereafter. With this deliberate invocation of ill we pass into spiritual darkness. The terror of it moves Albany rather than Goneril, whom, indeed, nothing is ever to move. But as he rouses himself to plead against it Lear is gone.[1]

Now havoc begins in him. We have his raging, distracted return, tears of helpless despair punctuating hysterical threats; later the stamping, muttering impatience of his wait for his horses. We

---

[1] The " Away, away," is thus spoken to Albany, and has no reference to the servants, who have already been sent off, nor to Lear's own departure. The point is disputable, no doubt, and I would not go to the stake for my reading of it. The Quartos have " Go, go, my people " repeated, as if his first order had not been obeyed. I must leave it to better judges of their origin and value to say whether this is mere muddlement of text. But, even if it is not, the Folio's change of phrase might cover a change of meaning too.

know that he sets out on a long hard ride, dinnerless after his hunting. Later we learn that the journey was wasted; he had to post on to Gloucester's. Did he ride through the night without rest or pause? Shakespeare is hunting Lear and the play's action hard and using every device to do it.

Yet the next day when he reaches Gloucester's house—this old man past eighty, and physically we should suppose near exhaustion—he is master of himself, is his most regal self again.[1] We are given the scene with Kent awaked in the stocks to show it.

> Ha!
> Makest thou this shame thy pastime?

All the old dignity in this; there follows the brusque familiar give and take which true authority never fears to practise with its dependents; then again the majestic

> Resolve me, with all modest haste, which way
> Thou might'st deserve, or they impose, this usage
> Coming from us,

and the iron self-control in which the shameful tale is heard. When the tale is ended he still stands silent, while the Fool pipes for us an artless mockery (the art of this!) of his bitter and ominous thoughts. Regan too, Regan too! The grief of disillusion has now become physical pain to him. But he masters it.

> Where is this daughter? . . .
> Follow me not; stay here.

[1] The outward signs of exhaustion must begin to be upon him.

And, solitary in his pride, he goes to face and prove the worst.

If the play, with the invocation of the curse upon Goneril, entered an arena of anarchy and darkness, Lear himself is to pass now from personal grievance to the taking upon him, as great natures may, of the imagined burden of the whole world's sorrow—and if his nature breaks under it, what wonder! And Shakespeare brings about this transition from malediction to martyrdom with great art, by contrivance direct and indirect, by strokes broad and subtle; nor ever—his art in this at its greatest—does he turn his Lear from a man into an ethical proposition. The thing is achieved—as the whole play is achieved—in terms of humanity, and according to the rubric of drama.

Lear comes back with Gloucester; the well-meaning Gloucester, whose tact is the one thing least likely to placate him. He is struggling with himself, with the old tyrannic temper, with his new-found knowledge of himself, with his body's growing weakness. He is like a great oak-tree, torn at the roots, blown this way and that. When the half-veiled insolence of Regan's and Cornwall's greeting should affront him, a pathetic craving for affection peeps through. When he once more finds refuge in irony, the edge of it is turned against himself. But with four quick shocks—his sudden recall of the outrage upon his servant, the sound of a trumpet, the sight of Oswald, the sight of Goneril—he is brought to a stand and to face the realities arrayed against him. The confronting must be made very plain to us. On the one side stand Goneril and Regan and

Cornwall in all authority. The perplexed
Gloucester hovers a little apart. On the other
side is Lear, the Fool at his feet, and his one
servant, disarmed, free but a minute, behind
him. Things are at their issue. His worst errors,
after all, have partaken of nobility; he has
scorned policy. He has given himself, helpless,
into these carnal hands. He will abide, then, as
nobly the fate he has courted. Note the single
touch of utter scorn for the cur Cornwall, who, the
moment looking likely, takes credit for those stocks.

> I set him there, sir; but his own disorders
> Deserved much less advancement
> You! Did you!

But all consequences he'll abide, he'll welcome
even, abjure his curses, run from one ingrate
daughter to the other, implore and bargain, till
the depth is sounded and he stands at last sur-
rendered, and level in his helplessness and depriva-
tion with the least of his fellow-men.

Goneril.   Hear me, my lord,
What need you five-and-twenty, ten, or five
To follow in a house where twice so many
Have a command to tend you?
Regan.   What need one?
Lear.   O! reason not the need; our basest beggars
Are in the poorest thing superfluous:
Allow not nature more than nature needs,
Man's life is cheap as beast's. . . .
                    But, for true need—
You heavens, give me that patience, patience I
need!
You see me here, you gods, a poor old man
As full of grief as age, wretched in both!

" O! reason not the need . . ."! This abandon-
ing of the struggle and embracing of misfortune

is a turning-point of the play, a salient moment in the development of Lear's character, and its significance must be marked. He is now at the nadir of his fortunes; the tragic heights are at hand.

It may be thought that by emphasising so many minor points of stagecraft the great outlines of play and character are obscured. But while Shakespeare projects greatly, asking from his interpreters a simplicity of response, lending them greatness by virtue of this convention that passes the play's material through the sole crucible of their speech and action, he yet saves them alive, so to speak—not stultified in an attempt to overpass their own powers nor turned to mere mouthpieces of mighty lines—by constant references to the commonplace (we noted more of them in discussing the methods of the dialogue). He invigorates his play's action by keeping its realities upon a battleground where any and every sort of stroke may tell.

Thus there now follows the tense passage in which Goneril, Regan and Cornwall snuff the impending storm and find good reason for ill-doing. What moralists! Regan with her

> O! sir, to wilful men,
> The injuries that they themselves procure
> Must be their schoolmasters.

Cornwall, with his

> Shut up your doors, my lord; 'tis a wild night:
> My Regan counsels well; come out of the storm.

This is surely the very voice—though the tones may be harsh, perhaps—of respectability and common sense? And what a prelude to the

'high engender'd' battle to come! Before the
battle is joined, though, Kent also intervenes;
to keep the play's story going its more pedestrian
way and to steady us against the imaginative
turmoil pending. This use of Kent is masterly;
and the contrasting use of the Fool, feeble, fantastic, pathetic, a foil to Lear, a foil to the storm—
what more incongruous sight conceivable than such
a piece of court tinsel so drenched and buffeted!
—is more than masterly. But Lear's own progress is the thing, his passing from that royal
defiance of the storm to the welcomed shelter of
the hovel. He passes by the road of patience:

> No, I will be the pattern of all patience;
> I will say nothing,

of thankfulness that he is at last

>   . . . a man
> More sinn'd against than sinning,

to the gentleness of

>   My wits begin to turn.
> Come on, my boy. How dost, my boy? Art cold?
> I am cold myself. Where is this straw, my fellow?
> The art of our necessities is strange
> That can make vile things precious. Come, your hovel,

and, a little later yet, mind and body still further
strained towards breaking point, to the gentle
dignity, when Kent would make way for him—to
the more than kingly dignity of—

> Prithee, go in thyself: seek thine own ease.
> This tempest will not give me leave to ponder
> On things would hurt me more. But I'll go in:
> In, boy; go first.[1]

---

[1] There are practical reasons for postponing the entering
of the hovel by a scene. For Kent to lead Lear elsewhere
fits both with the agitated movement of the action and the

Now comes the crowning touch of all:

> I'll pray, and then I'll sleep.

In the night's bleak exposure he will yet kneel down, like a child at bedtime, to pray.

> Poor naked wretches, wheresoe'er you are,
> That bide the pelting of this pitiless storm,
> How shall your houseless heads and unfed sides,
> Your loop'd and window'd raggedness, defend you
> From seasons such as these? O, I have ta'en
> Too little care of this! Take physic, pomp;
> Expose thyself to feel what wretches feel;
> That thou mayst shake the superflux to them,
> And show the heavens more just.

To this haven of the spirit has he come, the Lear of unbridled power and pride. And how many dramatists, could they have achieved so much, would have been content to leave him here! Shakespeare himself, in some earlier phase of his artistry, might have done so. Those that like their drama rounded and trim may speculate upon a finish according to the canons of such art. A play more compassable in performance would result, no doubt. But the wind of a harsher doctrine is blowing through Shakespeare now. Criticism is apt to fix upon the episode of the

---

freedom of Elizabethan stage method. It enables Shakespeare both to relieve the high tension of the storm scenes and to provide for the continuity of the Gloucester–Edmund story. And he takes advantage of all this to show us some further battering at Lear's sanity. Note in particular the ominously broken thoughts and sentences of the end of the speech to Kent just before the hovel is reached; and these, as ominously, are set between connected, reasoned passages.

storm as the height of his attempt and the point of his defeat; but it is this storm of the mind here beginning upon which he expends skill and imagination most recklessly till inspiration has had its will of him; and the drama of desperate vision ensuing it is hard indeed for actors to reduce to the positive medium of their art—and not reduce it to ridicule. The three coming scenes of Lear's madness are Shakespeare at his boldest. They pass beyond the needs of the plot, they belong to a far larger synthesis.[1] For once, little question as between platform stage and picture stage comes into the interpreting. Lest we imagine any such handicap, let us look the more closely into the technical means by which they are made effective.

The boldest and simplest of these is the provision of Poor Tom, that living instance of all rejection. Here, under our eyes, is Lear's new vision of himself.

> What! have his daughters brought him to this pass?
> Could'st thou save nothing? Did'st thou give them all?

Side by side stand the noble old man, and the naked, scarce human wretch.

> Is man no more than this? Consider him well. Thou owest the worm no silk, the beast no hide, the sheep no wool, the cat no perfume. Ha! here's three on's are sophisticated; thou art the thing itself; unaccommodated man is no more but such a poor, bare, forked animal as thou art. Off, off, you lendings! Come; unbutton here.

---

[1] It is worth noting that the Folio cuts out the lunatic trial of Regan and Goneril. Was it, by chance, this episode that Shakespeare's actors failed to make effective, while the scenes of the storm were of no particular difficulty to them?

Here is a world of argument epitomised as only drama can epitomise it, flashed on us by word and action. Into this, one might add, has Shakespeare metamorphosed those old Moralities, which were the infancy of his art.

> What! hath your grace no better company?

gasps poor Gloucester, bewailing at once the King's wrongs and his own, as he offers shelter from the storm. But Lear, now all calm, will only pace up and down, arm in arm with this refuse of humanity.

> Noble philosopher, your company.

Nor will he seek shelter without him. So they reach the outhouse, all of his own castle that Gloucester dare offer. What a group! Kent, sturdy and thrifty of words; Gloucester, tremulous; the bedraggled and exhausted Fool; and Lear, magnificently courteous and deliberate, keeping close company with his gibbering fellow-man.[1]

They are in shelter. Lear is silent; till the Fool, himself never overfitted, we may suppose, in body or mind for the rough and tumble of the world, rallies, as if to celebrate their safety, to a semblance of his old task. Edgar, for his own safety's sake, must play Poor Tom to the life now. Kent has his eyes on his master; he hears him rave, watches him at what new fantastic trick! The old king is setting two joint stools side by side; they are Regan and Goneril, and the Fool and the beggar are to pass judgment upon them.

[1] And Kent is unknown to Lear and Edgar to his father, as we shall sufficiently remember.

This mad mummery of the trial comes near to being something we might call pure drama— as one speaks of pure mathematics or pure music— in the sense that it cannot be rendered into other terms than its own. The sound of the dialogue matters more than its meaning. Poor Tom and the Fool chant antiphonally; Kent's deep and kindly tones tell against the high agonised voice of Lear, melodious in verse or turning to the hard certitude of prose. But the significance is in the show. Where Lear once sat in his majesty, there sit the Fool and the outcast with Kent that he banished beside them; while he, witless, musters his failing strength to beg justice upon a joint stool. Was there more justice done, asks the picture, when Lear himself sat there in majesty and sanity and power?

This is pure drama in that its effect can only be gained by due combination of sound, sight and meaning, acting directly upon the sensibility of the audience. And what could be more eloquent of Lear's release from the sequences and arithmetic of life than the picture of his mind presented in these terms, themselves divorced from all pedestrian reasoning and reason? But what, as far as Lear is concerned, is to follow? You cannot, one would say, continue the development of a character in the language of lunacy—of darkness, illumined though it may be by the most brilliant flashes of lightning. Will not even such another scene come as an anti-climax? Yet Shakespeare is to give us such another. A redundant scene, as far as the needs of the story go; nor could we complain that Lear's character was left

178

incomplete if he passed from the falling into exhausted sleep upon the poor bed in the outhouse to his waking to find Cordelia by his side. But it will lift the play's argument to a still rarer height.

Patent anti-climax is avoided by keeping Lear from the stage for a long time. A short scene serves, after a while, to remind us of him, to tell us he is still out of his wits, and, very vaguely— since, indeed, Shakespeare might be hard put to it for precision—where he is and why.[1] But when he enters, *mad*—though not *fantastically dressed with wild flowers*, which is an eighteenth-century addi- tion—we still may well find ourselves asking: What now, and what more?

The larger dramatic value of a meeting between the mad Lear and blind Gloucester it is surely hard to overrate. What could better point the transcendent issue Shakespeare has developed from the two old stories than this encounter of the sensual man robbed of his eyes with the wilful man, the light of his mind put out? The situation is not left to its own eloquence as is that of the mock trial; the moral is drawn as clearly as need be, while the very nature of the scene keeps it from being deadened by edification. For a guide to the simpler souls among the audience we have the sympathetic Edgar with a couple of asides; the first to counteract ridicule, if there's a risk of that, the second a clear under- lining of the scene's purpose. This apart, Lear is oracular, and Gloucester in his simple helplessness is eloquent of himself. And even as in life we must snatch what meaning we may from the chaos of passion and mad purpose the tragic world seems

[1] For the question of text involved, see p. 228.

to be; so, fitfully and poignantly, is it brought home to us here.

They flattered me like a dog. . . . To say 'ay' and 'no' to everything I said! . . . When the rain came to wet me once and the wind to make me chatter, when the thunder would not peace at my bidding, there I found 'em, there I smelt 'em out. Go to, they are not men o' their words: they told me I was everything; 'tis a lie, I am not ague-proof.

Then, as he fixes Gloucester with eyes as unseeing as his:

> What was thy cause?
> Adultery?
> Thou shalt not die: die for adultery! No:
> The wren goes to't, and the small gilded fly
> Does lecher in my sight.
> Let copulation thrive; for Gloucester's bastard son
> Was kinder to his father than my daughters
> Got 'tween the lawful sheets.

But Gloucester knows the truth of that, we know! And there stands Edgar, known to us, still unknown to him!

Shakespeare takes a chance here, legitimately enough—for the mind of a madman runs thus, as do our own imaginations when bitterness loosens them—to attune us to Regan and Goneril in their new unfolding, their ripeness of ill. Then, sins of the flesh being scourged, Lear's madness scourges his own sin. Visions of judgment beset him; it is the fantasy of the mock trial finding phrases. But there is a difference. For, from his cry for vengeance upon the wicked, he has now passed to

. . see how yond justice rails upon yond simple thief. Hark, in thine ear; change places, and, handy-dandy,

180

which is the justice, which is the thief? Thou hast seen a
farmer's dog bark at a beggar?

Ay, sir.

And the creature run from the cur?   There thou mightest
behold the great image of authority; a dog's obeyed in
office.

Thou rascal beadle, hold thy bloody hand!
Why dost thou lash that whore?   Strip thine own back;
Thou hotly lust'st to use her in that kind
For which thou whipst her.   The usurer hangs the cozener.
Through tattered clothes small vices do appear;
Robes and furr'd gowns hide all.   Plate sin with gold,
And the strong lance of justice hurtless breaks;
Arm it in rags, a pigmy's straw does pierce it.

Shakespeare has led Lear through suffering to
compassion for the sinner as well as for the poor,
has led him mad to where he could not hope to
lead him sane—to where our own commonsense
will, of course, not let us follow him.

> None does offend, none, I say, none.

He has led him to a deep compassion upon mankind itself.

I know thee well enough; thy name is Gloucester;
Thou must be patient; we came crying hither:
Thou know'st the first time that we smell the air
We wawl and cry.   I will preach to thee: mark.

Alack, alack the day!

When we are born, we cry that we are come
To this great stage of fools.

This last scene of Lear's madness may be
redundant, then, to the strict action of the play,
but to its larger issues it is most germane.   It
is perhaps no part of the play that Shakespeare
set out to write.   The play that he found himself
writing would be how much the poorer without it!

The simple perfection of the scene that restores

Lear to Cordelia one can leave unsullied by comment. What need of any? Let the producer only note that there is reason in the Folio's stage direction:

Enter Lear in a chair carried by servants.

For when he comes to himself it is to find that he is royally attired and as if seated on his throne again. It is from this throne that he totters to kneel at Cordelia's feet.[1] Note, too, the pain of his response to Kent's

In your own kingdom, sir.
Do not abuse me.

Finally, Lear must pass from the scene with all the ceremony due to royalty; not mothered—please!—by Cordelia.

Cordelia found again and again lost, what is left for Lear but to die? But for her loss, however, his own death might seem to us an arbitrary stroke; since the old Lear, we may say, is already dead. Shakespeare, moreover, has transported him spiritually altogether beyond such issues as defeat, disgrace and disillusion. This is, perhaps, why the action of the battle which will seemingly defeat his fortunes is minimised. It is certainly the key to the meaning of the scene which follows. Cordelia, who would " out-frown false fortune's frown," is ready to face her sisters and to shame them—were there a chance of it!—with the sight of her father's wrongs. But Lear himself has no interest in anything of the sort.

---

[1] Shakespeare kept—and transformed—this piece of business from the old play; for Cordelia kneels, too, of course. It should be given its full value.

> No, no, no, no! Come let's away to prison.
> We two alone will sing like birds i' the cage:
> When thou dost ask me blessing, I'll kneel down,
> And ask of thee forgiveness: [1] so we'll live,
> And pray, and sing, and tell old tales and laugh
> At gilded butterflies, and hear poor rogues
> Talk of court news. . . .

He has passed beyond care for revenge or for victory, beyond the questioning of rights and wrongs. Better indeed to be oppressed, if so you can be safe from contention. Prison will bring him freedom.

> Upon such sacrifices, my Cordelia,
> The gods themselves throw incense. Have I caught thee?
> He that parts us shall bring a brand from heaven
> And fire us hence like foxes. Wipe thine eyes;
> The good years shall devour them, flesh and fell,
> Ere they shall make us weep: we'll see 'em starve first.

Lear's death, upon one ground or another, is artistically inevitable. Try to imagine his survival; no further argument will be needed. The death of Cordelia has been condemned as a wanton outrage upon our feelings and so as an æsthetic blot upon the play. But the dramatic mind that was working to the tune of

> As flies to wanton boys are we to the gods;
> They kill us for their sport,

was not likely to be troubled by niceties of sentiment or æsthetics. The main tragic truth about life, to the Shakespeare that wrote *King Lear*, was its capricious cruelty. And what meeter sacrifice to this than Cordelia? Besides, as we have seen, he must provide this new Lear with a tragic determinant, since "the great

---

[1] That scene in the old play haunted Shakespeare.

183

rage . . . is kill'd in him," which precipitated catastrophe for the old Lear. And what but Cordelia's loss would suffice?

We have already set Lear's last scene in comparison with his first; it will be worth while to note a little more particularly the likeness and the difference. The same commanding figure; he bears the body of Cordelia as lightly as ever he carried robe, crown and sceptre before. All he has undergone has not so bated his colossal strength but that he could kill with his bare hands the slave that murdered her. Albany, Edgar, Kent and the rest stand silent and intent around him; Regan and Goneril are there, silent too. He glares blankly at them. When speech is torn from him, in place of the old kingly rhetoric we have only the horrible, half human

Howl, howl, howl, howl!

Who these are, for all their dignity and martial splendour, for all the respect they show him, he neither knows nor cares. They are men of stone and murderous traitors; though, after a little, through the mist of his suffering, comes a word for Kent. All his world, of power and passion and will, and the wider world of thought over which his mind in its ecstasy had ranged, is narrowed now to Cordelia; and she is dead in his arms.

Here is the clue to the scene; this terrible concentration upon the dead, and upon the unconquerable fact of death. This thing was Cordelia; she was alive, she is dead. Here is human tragedy brought to its simplest terms, fit ending to a tragic play that has seemed to outleap human experience. From power of intellect and will, from the imaginative sweep of madness, Shakespeare brings Lear to this; to no moralising nor high thoughts, but just to

> She's gone for ever.
> I know when one is dead and when one lives;
> She's dead as earth. Lend me a looking-glass;
> If that her breath will mist or stain the stone,
> Why, then she lives.

Lacking a glass, he catches at a floating feather. That stirs on her lips; a last mockery. Kent kneels by him to share his grief. Then to the bystanders comes the news of Edmund's death; the business of life goes forward, as it will, and draws attention from him for a moment. But what does he heed? When they turn back to him he has her broken body in his arms again.

> And my poor fool is hang'd. No, no, no life!
> Why should a dog, a horse, a rat, have life,
> And thou no breath at all? Thou'lt come no more,
> Never, never, never, never, never!
> Pray you undo this button; thank you, sir.
> Do you see this? Look on her, look, her lips,
> Look there, look there! [1]

Goneril, Regan and Cordelia

Shakespeare's point of departure for all three is that of the crude old story. Moreover, with regard to Goneril and Regan he is quite content to assume—we shrink from the assumption now-adays—that there are really wicked people in the

---

[1] Bradley has an admirable note upon this passage, just such a fine piece of perception as we expect from him. Lear, he says, at the very last, thinks that Cordelia lives, and dies of the joy of it.

world. That admitted, these two exemplars of the fact are lifelike enough. Their aspect may be determined by the story's needs, but their significance does not end here; and, within the limits afforded them, they develop freely and naturally, each in her own way.

Likeness and difference are marked from the beginning. They are both realists. Their father wants smooth speech of them and they give it, echoing his very phrases and tones. They ignore Cordelia's reproaches; she is exiled and in disgrace, so they safely may. Left alone together (and the drop here from verse to prose seems to bring us with something of a bump to the plain truth about them), they are under no illusions at all, we find, about their own good fortune.

. . . he always loved our sister most; and with what poor judgment he hath now cast her off appears too grossly.

There are few things more unlovely than the passionless appraisement of evil and our profit in it. They are as wide-awake to the chances of trouble ahead; but while Regan would wait and see, Goneril means to go to meet it.

If the quarrel between King Lear and his two daughters had been brought into the law courts, counsels' speeches for Regan and Goneril would have been interesting. But what a good case Goneril makes for herself unaided! The setting on of Oswald to provoke Lear might, one supposes, have been kept out of the evidence. True, the reservation of a hundred knights was a definite condition of his abdication. But their behaviour was impeachable; it may well have been if Lear's own treatment of Oswald set them an example.

186

He was almost in his dotage; unbalanced, certainly. His outbursts of ironic rage, the cursing of Goneril, his subsequent ravings—his whole conduct shows him unfit to look after himself. For his own sake, then, how much better for his daughters' servants to wait on him! And Regan, though she needs Goneril's prompting, makes an even better case of it; the weaker nature is the more plausible. A jury of men and women of common-sense might well give their verdict against Lear; and we can hear the judge ruling upon the one point of law in his favour with grave misgiving that he is doing him no good. How then can we call Regan and Goneril double-dyed fiends? They played the hypocrite for a kingdom; but which of us might not? Having got what they wanted and more than they expected they found excellent excuse for not paying the price for it. Like failings have been known in the most reputable people. Their conduct so far, it could be argued, has been eminently respectable, level-headed and worldly-wise. They do seem somewhat hard-hearted, but that is all. That is all!

Is there any cause in nature that makes these hard hearts?

But from now on the truth about them grows patent. Does prosperity turn their heads? It releases hidden devils. When Gloucester's defection is discovered they waste no words.

Hang him instantly.
Pluck out his eyes.

And the weaker Regan grows the more violent of the two; she turns crueller even than that

187

KING LEAR

bloody wolf, Cornwall, her husband. For amid the scuffling a little later she can think to tell Gloucester that his own son has betrayed him; and even as he faces her, blinded and bleeding, she can jeer at him.

The devil of lust comes now to match with the devil of cruelty. Goneril has hardly seen Edmund but she marks him down with those

> . . . strange œilliads and most speaking looks

—which rouse Regan to jealousy as quickly. In their plot upon their father they were clever enough, self-controlled, subtle. But, the beast let loose in them, they turn reckless, shameless, foolish. Regan, with a little law on her side, presumes on it; so Goneril poisons her as she might a rat. And the last note of Goneril is one of devilish pride.

> Say, if I do, the laws are mine, not thine:
> Who can arraign me for it?

Flinging this at her husband when he confronts her with the proof that she meant to have his life, she departs to take her own.

We may see, then, in Goneril and Regan, evil triumphant, self-degrading and self-destructive. It may also be that, from beginning to end, Shakespeare, for his part, sees little to choose between hot lust and murdering hand and the hard heart, in which all is rooted.

It will be a fatal error to present Cordelia as a meek saint. She has more than a touch of her father in her. She is as proud as he is, and as obstinate, for all her sweetness and her youth. And, being young, she answers uncalculatingly

188

with pride to his pride even as later she answers
with pity to his misery. To miss this likeness
between the two is to miss Shakespeare's first
important dramatic effect; the mighty old man
and the frail child, confronted, and each un-
yielding.

> So young and so untender?
> So young, my lord, and true.

And they both have the right of it, after all. If
age owes some tolerance to youth, it may be
thought too that youth owes to age and father-
hood something more—and less—than the truth.
But she has courage, has Cordelia, amazing
courage. Princess though she be, it is no small
matter to stand her ground before Lear, throned
in the plenitude of his power, to stand up to him
without effort, explanation, or excuse. Nor does
she wince at the penalty, nor to the end utter one
pleading word. Nor, be it noted, does Kent,
who is of her temper, ask pity for her. His chief
concern is to warn Lear against his own folly and
its consequences.[1] It is her strength of mind he
emphasises and praises.

> The gods to their dear shelter take thee, maid,
> That justly think'st and hast most rightly said!

Nor would she, apparently, open her mouth again
to her father but that she means her character
shall be cleared. And even this approach to him
is formal and uncompromising:

> I yet beseech your majesty . . .

[1] And certain small alterations from Quarto to Folio
emphasise this.

She does (Shakespeare keeps her human) slip in, as if it hardly mattered, a dozen words of vindication:

> . . . since what I well intend
> I'll do't before I speak.

Yet, lest even that should seem weakness, she nullifies its effect for a finish. Nor does Lear respond, nor exonerate her except by a noncommittal growl. Still, she is not hard.

> The jewels of our father, with wash'd eyes
> Cordelia leaves you. . . .

Shakespeare has provided in this encounter between Cordelia and Lear that prime necessity of drama, clash of character; that sharpest clash, moreover, of like in opposition to like. He has added wonder and beauty by setting these twin spirits in noble and contrasted habitations. Pride unchecked in Lear has grown monstrous and diseased with his years. In her youth it shows unspoiled, it is in flower. But it is the same pride.

The technical achievement in Shakespeare's staging of Cordelia is his gain of a maximum effect by a minimum of means. It is a triumph of what may be called placing. The character itself has, to begin with, that vitality which positive virtues give. Cordelia is never in doubt about herself; she has no vagaries, she is what she is all circumstances apart, what she says seems to come new-minted from her mind, and our impression of her is as clean cut. Add to this her calm and steadfast isolation among the contending or subservient figures of that first scene—and the fact, of course, that from this very thrift of herself the broadcast violence of the play's whole action springs—then we see how, with but a reminder of her here and there, Shakespeare could trust to her reappearance after long delay, no jot of her importance nor of our interest in her bated. Indeed, if the Folio text gives us in the main his own reconsiderations, he found his first care to reinstate her in our sympathy a scene before she reappears to be needless.[1] But at this point the play itself is beginning to have need of her return. Somehow its intolerable agonies must be brought to rest; and amid the dreadful flux our memory of her certainty abides.

There is not, at any time, much to explain in Cordelia. Nor does she now herself protest her love and expand her forgiveness. She has not changed; elaboration would only falsify her. Not that she is by nature taciturn; she can resolve the harmonies of her mind, and Shakespeare gives a flowing music to them.

> Was this a face
> To be opposed against the warring winds?
> To stand against the deep dread-bolted thunder?
> In the most terrible and nimble stroke
> Of quick cross lightning? to watch—poor perdu!
> With this thin helm? Mine enemy's dog,
> Though he had bit me, should have stood that night
> Against my fire.

But even this is not spoken to Lear. To him she still says little. It is as if speech itself were not a simple or genuine enough thing for the expressing of her deep heart. And her

> No cause, no cause!

when he would welcome her reproaches, is not at all the kindly, conventional, superior " Let's for-

[1] Act IV, Scene iii.

get it " of the morally offended. It is but the complement of that " Nothing " which cost her a kingdom, and as true of her in its tenderness as the other was true. For the simple secret of Cordelia's nature is that she does not see things from the standpoint of her own gain or loss. She did not beg, she does not bargain. She can give as she could lose, keeping a quiet mind. It is no effort to her to love her father better than herself. Yet this supremest virtue, as we count it, is no gain to him; we must note this too. Her wisdom of heart showed her Regan and Goneril as they were; yet it was an inarticulate wisdom and provoked evil in Lear, and could but hold her bound in patience till the evil was purged. Is there, then, an impotence in such goodness, lovely as we find it? And is this why Shakespeare lets her slip out of the play a few scenes later to her death, as if, for all her beauty of spirit, she were not of so much account? Neither good fortune nor ill can touch Cordelia herself; this is her strength and her weakness both.

> For thee, oppressed king, am I cast down;
> Myself could else outfrown false fortune's frown,

she says; and so she could, we are sure. Then she falls into dumbness—into such a dumbness as was her first undoing—and passes, silent, from our sight.

Kent

Here is another positive, absolute being; he, Lear and Cordelia make a trinity of them. He has not Lear's perilous intellect nor Cordelia's peace of soul. His dominant quality is his unquestioning courage; akin to this the selflessness

192

which makes it as easy for him to be silent as to speak. And he springs from Shakespeare's imagination all complete; full-flavoured and consistent from the first. Surer sign yet of his author's certainty about him is the natural inconsistency of the man as we see him. Through the first three acts there is never a stroke in the drawing of Kent which is merely conventional, nor yet an uncertain one. But neither is there one which, however unexpected, need perplex us. And for a small sign of Shakespeare's confidence in the sufficiency of his creature, see the shrewd critical thrust which he lets Cornwall have at him:

> This is some fellow,
> Who, having been praised for bluntness, doth affect
> A saucy roughness. . . .

Even though it be a Cornwall disparaging a Kent, the thrust is shrewd enough for Shakespeare not to risk it unless he is confident that Kent's credit with the audience is firm.

This variety and apparent inconsistency gives great vitality. From the Kent of the first scene, quick of eye, frank at a question:

> Is not this your son, my lord?

impatient at half answers:

> I cannot conceive you,

yet tolerant, discreetly courteous, dry, self-contained:

> I cannot wish the fault undone, the issue of it being so proper;

but gentle and kindly too:

> I must love you and sue to know you better

—from this we pass without warning to the impetuous outburst against Lear; and unmannerly though this may be, it is still dignified, collected, and cool. From this to the Kent of the borrowed accents,—but never more himself than in his disguise—to the man of

> What would'st thou?
> Service.
> Who would'st thou serve?
> You.
> Dost thou know me, fellow?
> No, sir; but you have that in your countenance which I would fain call master.
> What's that?
> Authority,

to the Kent of the tripping of Oswald; and, at their next meeting, with Oswald so unwary as to ask him

> What dost thou know me for?

to the Kent of

> A knave, a rascal, an eater of broken meats; a base, proud, shallow, beggarly, three-suited, hundred-pound, filthy, worsted-stocking knave; a lily-livered, action-taking knave; a whoreson, glass-gazing, super-serviceable, finical rogue; a one-trunk inheriting slave; one that wouldst be a bawd in way of good service, and art nothing but the composition of a knave, beggar, coward, pandar, and the son and heir of a mongrel bitch; one whom I will beat into clamorous whining if thou deniest the least syllable of thy addition,

to the resourceful, humorous disputant of the scene with Cornwall and Regan, and to the philosopher in the stocks, with his

> Fortune, good-night; smile once more; turn thy wheel.

Having so opulently endowed him with life, Shakespeare, we may say, can now afford to be thriftier of attention to him for a little; he had better be, we might add, or the balance of the play's interest will go awry. But it is of a piece with the character that, when misfortune overwhelms Lear, Kent should sink himself in it, that his colourfulness should fade, his humour wane, and the rest of the play find him tuned to this one key of vigilant unquestioning service; till he comes to the final simplicity of

> I have a journey, sir, shortly to go.
> My master calls me, I must not say no.

Nevertheless Shakespeare does seem in Act IV to lose interest in him, thus straitened, and he keeps him a place in the action carelessly enough. Throughout the storm scenes, of course, his sober, single-minded concern for the King does but reinforce his dramatic credit; it is, besides, a necessary check to their delirium. He could have even less to say here, and his very presence would be a strength. It is like Kent not to fuss as poor Gloucester fusses, not to talk when he need not, to think of the morrow and do the best he can meanwhile. Shakespeare allows him—a just economy—two flashes of emotion; the first when Lear turns to him with

> Wilt break my heart?
> I'd rather break my own,

he says. And once—

> O pity!

No more than that.

It is after he has taken Lear to Dover that, as a character, he begins to live upon the credit of his

14

past. Shakespeare seems not quite sure what
more he may want of him; he only does not
want him to complicate with his vigorous
personality the crowded later action of the
play. What his purpose may be in sustaining
his disguise—

> Pardon, dear madam;
> Yet to be known shortens my made intent:
> My boon I make it that you know me not
> Till time and I think meet

—is never very clear. But Shakespeare's own
purpose here is clear enough; not to spoil Lear's
reconciliation with Cordelia, by adding to it a
recognition of Kent. The couplet with which
Kent ends the scene:

> My point and period will be throughly wrought,
> Or well or ill, as this day's battle fought,

has in the event neither much significance nor
consequence. It is a safe remark and sounds
well. We might suppose (we may do so, if we
like; but in fact an audience will not stop to
consider a commentator's point) that Kent is
counting, if Lear is defeated, on serving him still
in disguise, when known he could not. But he
does not appear in the battle or the defeat; and
this we might think (if, again, we stopped to think;
but while the play is acting we shall not) as
strange as his neglect which had let Lear escape
to wander

> As mad as the vex'd sea; singing aloud . . .

But the simple explanation is that Shakespeare
finds he has no more dramatic use for Kent till

he can bring him on, the play all but done,
with

> I am come
> To bid my king and master aye good-night.

So he must just keep him in being meanwhile.

That Kent should survive as effectively to the
play's end is at once a tribute to the vitality of
his first projection and to the tact with which
Shakespeare can navigate the shallows of his art.
And the actor who can express himself and impress
himself upon us as well by silence as by speech
will find no difficulties in the part.[1]

The Fool

The Fool can never, of course, be to us what
he was to the play's first audience. For them,
Shakespeare's achievement lay in the double conversion of a stock stage character and a traditional Court figure to transcendent dramatic use.
There are few greater pleasures in art than to
find the familiar made new; but to us stage Fool
and Court Fool alike are strange to start with.
Court Fool has, to be sure, a likely claim to a
place in the play, and can claim a place too in

---

[1] If it be said that there is nothing in the Kent of Act IV
which, upon analysis, belies his character, yet this preface
is concerned also with his presentment, and that is ineffective
and even halting. But what of his sudden outburst in
Act IV, Sc. iii:

> It is the stars;
> The stars above us, govern our conditions;

—is this the authentic Kent? And even if Shakespeare
were here starting to develop a new phase of the man, he
never goes on.

For a masterly analysis of the whole character we should
turn to A. C. Bradley's lecture on *King Lear*.

our historical consciousness. Grant the old King such a favourite: it is good character scheming to contrast his royal caprices with such spaniel affection; dramatic craft at its best to leave Lear in adversity this one fantastic remnant of royalty. This, and much more of intrinsic value, we cannot lose. But what, from the transcended stage Fool, did Shakespeare gain besides?

Elizabethan acting did not inhabit the removed footlight-defended stage of the theatre of to-day, and all its technique and conventions and the illusion it created differ appropriately in consequence; this is the constant theme of these prefaces, and must be of any study of the staging of Shakespeare's plays. But certain effects, however gained, are common to all drama, certain problems recur. A problem in the writing and acting of tragedy is the alternate creating and relaxing of emotional strain; the tenser the strain, the less long can an audience appreciatively endure it. 'Comic relief' has a crude sound; but, to some degree and in some form or other, the thing it suggests is a necessity. Greek tragedy had 'choric relief'; emotion in the Greek theatre was magnified and rarefied at once, and sharp transitions were neither wanted nor workable. Shakespeare had the constant shift of scene and subject, usual in his theatre, to help him; and his most strenuous scenes, we may remark, tend to be short ones.[1] We may suppose him ever

[1] This play apart, they are noticeably so in *Macbeth* and in *Antony and Cleopatra*. In *Hamlet* and in *Othello* it may be said they are not. But in *Hamlet* the action is—and characteristically—not consistently strenuous; and the sustaining of the anguish in *Othello* is typical of the tragedy, helps give us the heroic measure of Othello himself.

mindful of the difficulty of keeping the attention of a motley audience fixed, but still alert; and in the body of a scene, if it needs must be a long one, we shall always find what may be called points of rest and recovery.

But the problem can be stated in other terms. Tragedy, it may be said, takes us out of ourselves; how else can it be enjoyed? A dash of comedy will, by contrast, restore us to ourselves; yet, for the tragedy's sake, the less conscious of the process we are the better. Here lay for Shakespeare, in this play, the histrionic value of the Fool. He wanted no comic relief in the crude sense; but the familiar stage figure, even though turned to tragic purpose, kept for that audience, if insensibly, its traditional hail-fellow quality. Only the dramatic and human value of the character is preserved us for to-day to the full. Of the effect of the snatches of song and rhyme, the lyric lightening of the epic strength of these scenes, we keep only the most manifest part. The things themselves are queer to us, and this is just what they should not be. And of the friendly feeling, the sense of being at ease with ourselves, which the stage Fool, a-straddle between play and audience, could create for the Elizabethans, we save nothing at all. We have felt something of the sort as children perhaps, when, at the Panto-mime, after the removed mysteries of the trans-formation scene, came the harlequinade and the clown, cuddling us up to him with his " Here we are again." It may seem a far cry from red-hot poker and sausages to *King Lear*. But these indigenous attributes of the Fool are the under-lying strength of the part once its acting is in question; and it is Shakespeare's use and restraint and disguise of them at once that is so masterly. Out went the character, as we know, from the eighteenth-century versions of the play; nor actors nor audience, it was thought, could countenance such an aberration. Macready restored it with many misgivings and gave it to a girl to act. The producer to-day faces another difficulty. He finds a Fool all etherealised by the higher criticism. His first care, in the part's embodying, must be to see restored as much as may be of its lost aboriginal strength. Its actor must sing like a lark, juggle his words so that the mere skill delights us, and tumble around with all the grace in the world. Satisfy these simpler demands, and the subtleties will have their effect; neglect them, and you might as well try to play tunes on a punctured organ stop.

About the Fool's character in the personal sense there is really not much to be said, though it is a subject upon which the romantic commentator has rejoiced to embroider his own fancies. Shakespeare, having had his use of the Fool, drops him incontinently; this alone might label the part of incidental, of decorative importance to the scheme of the play. But even this he makes a measure of the human pathos of the creature. We are told by the attendant knight before ever we see him:

Since my young lady's going into France, sir, the Fool hath much pined away.

No more of that; I have noted it well,

Lear answers (lest we should not note it well enough). But not a word more; above all never a hint from this professional jester himself that he has, or has a right to, any feelings of his own. His jests have grown bitterer lately perhaps; yet, for compensation, he is more full of song than ever. And come weal, come woe, he sticks to his job, sticks to it and to his master till the storm batters him into silence. With a ha'porth of warmth and comfort in him, he flickers bravely into jest again. But his task is done now, and he himself pretty well done for. He tells us so in a very short and bitter jest indeed:

> And I'll go to bed at noon.

And this is the last we hear or see of him; and what happens to him thereafter, who knows or cares? Which is quite according to the jesters'—and players'—code of professional honour, and to the common reward of its observance, as Shakespeare, of all men, would know well. To pursue the Fool beyond the play's bounds, to steep him in extraneous sentiment, is to miss the most characteristically dramatic thing about him.

One minor point about the part is yet an important one. The soliloquy with which Act III, Scene ii is made to end is certainly spurious.[1] Its own incongruity can be left out of the question; its offence against the dramatic situation disallows it. The very heart of this is Lear's new-found care for the shivering drenched creature at his side.

> Come on, my boy. How dost, my boy? Art cold . . .
> Poor fool and knave, I have one part in my heart
> That's sorry yet for thee.

[1] And surely it is time that all editions of Shakespeare put certain passages, whose fraud can be agreed upon, in expurgatorial brackets. We are ready for another—and another sort of—Bowdler.

Shakespeare is incapable—so would any other dramatist in his senses be—of stultifying himself by despatching Lear from the scene immediately after, and letting him leave the Fool behind him.

Gloucester, Edgar and Edmund

Gloucester and his sons are opposite numbers, as the phrase now goes, to Lear and his daughters. Gloucester himself is the play's nearest approach to the average sensual man. The civilised world is full of Gloucesters. In half a dozen short speeches Shakespeare sets him fully before us: turning elderly but probably still handsome; nice of speech if a little pompous; the accomplished courtier (he seems to be Lear's master of ceremonies); vain, as his mock modesty shows, but the joking shamelessness that succeeds it is mainly swagger; an egotist, and blind, knowing least of what he should know most, of his own two sons.

He hath been out nine years, and away he shall again.

That carelessly jovial sentence of banishment for Edmund proves his own death-sentence. Still, who could suspect the modest young newcomer, making his bow with

Sir, I shall study deserving,

of having such unpleasant thoughts in mind? Gloucester, like so many sensual men, is good-nature itself, as long as things go their easy, natural way; but when they fail to he is upset, rattled. Kent's banishment, the quarrel with Cordelia and France, and the King's utter reck-lessness set his mind off at one tangent and another and make him an easier victim to very simple deceit. We must not, however, appraise either his simplicity or Edgar's, at this moment, with detachment—for by that light, no human being, it would seem, between infancy and dotage, could be so gullible. Shakespeare asks us to allow him the fact of the deception, even as we have allowed him Lear's partition of the kingdom. It is his starting-point, the dramatist's 'let's pretend,' which is as essential to the beginning of a play as a 'let it be granted' to a proposition of Euclid. And, within bounds, the degree of pretence makes surprisingly little difference. It is what the assumption will commit him to that counts; once a play's action is under way it must develop as logically as Euclid, and far more logically than life. The art of the thing is to reward the spectator for his concession by never presuming on it; one should rather dress up the unlikely in the likelier. Thus Shakespeare makes Gloucester, with his pother about " these late eclipses of the sun and moon," the sort of man who might at any moment be taken in by any sort of tale; the more improbable, indeed, the better. He makes Edmund plausible even if the incriminating letter is not. And what better way to confirm a nervous, puzzled, opinionated man in an error than to reason calmly with him against it? Your victim will instinctively take the opposite point of view and forget that this was yours to begin with.[1] Does not the credulous nature

---

[1] But it follows that upon these lines we cannot be brought to a very close knowledge of Edgar too. Give him the same scope, and he must either get on the track of the truth or prove himself as great a fool as his father. So Shakespeare now and at his next appearance, does as little

crave to be deceived? Moreover, Shakespeare's first concern is to develop character, to put us on terms with these people; not till that is done, he knows, will their doings and sufferings really affect us. So it suits him, in any case, to sub-ordinate, for a little, what they do to what they are. And we part from Gloucester in this scene knowing him pretty thoroughly.

The sensual man does not stand up well against blows dealt to his complacent affections. Dis-illusion leaves Gloucester not only wax in Edmund's hands but more helpless than it belongs to him to be—fair-weather sailor though he has ever been!—in the alien troubles that now centre round him. Shakespeare's manœuvring of him through these scenes—from the welcome to the " noble arch and patron " to the moment when his guest's honoured fingers are plucking at his eyes—is a good example of the fruitful economy with which, once a character has ' come alive,' its simplest gesture, its very muteness is made significant. And Gloucester has been alive from the beginning; no illustration for a thesis, but unself-consciously himself. This very unself-con-sciousness is turned later to tragic account. Fate's worst revenge on him is that, blinded, he

---

with him as possible. This delays—and dangerously—our gaining interest in him. But a play survives sins of omission when the smallest sin of commission may damn it. Besides, time is valuable; and a sub-plot cannot, for the moment, be spared much more. The likelihood of the detail of this traffic between father and sons, the sending of letters, the "retire with me to my lodging . . . there's my key " and the rest, depends somewhat upon the large, loose organisa-tion of a great nobleman's household of that day, of which Shakespeare's audience would know well enough.

comes to see himself so clearly as he is, and to find the world, which once went so comfortably with him, a moral chaos. We might wonder at the amount of agonised reflection in this kind allotted to him. But mark its culmination:

> The King is mad: how stiff is my vile sense
> That I stand up, and have ingenious feeling
> Of my huge sorrows! Better I were distract:
> So should my thoughts be sever'd from my griefs,
> And woes by wrong imaginations lose
> The knowledge of themselves.

The one thing, it seems, that the average sensual man cannot endure is knowledge of the truth. Better death or madness than that!

Yet which of us must not feelingly protest that the Gloucester, who threads and fumbles his way so well-meaningly about the family battle-field his house is turned into (much against his will), is very harshly used indeed? Is this poetic justice? He does all that one who respects his superiors may do to save Kent from the ignominy of the stocks. He does his best to pacify Lear.

> I would have all well betwixt you.

How familiar is that heart-felt cry of the man who sees no sense in a quarrel! When he does take sides his reasons and his method are not heroic, it is true.

> These injuries the King now bears will be revenged home; there is part of a power already footed; we must incline to the King. I will look to him and privily relieve him, go you and maintain talk with the duke, that my charity be not of him perceived. If he asks for me, I am ill and gone to bed.

No, truly, it is not heroic, when battle is joined, to be ill and go to bed. But caution is a sort of a virtue; and the keeping of a family foot in each camp has good sanction. Yet who can be altogether wise?

If I die of it (he says in the next breath) as no less is threatened me, the King, my old master, must be relieved.

And this his best impulse is his undoing. In all innocence he points Edmund the way to his betrayal; Edmund has but to follow it—just a little further. Irony deepens when later he calls upon Cornwall to spare him in the sacred name of that hospitality which he himself has so spinelessly betrayed. Yet, " tied to the stake," he can "stand the course" courageously enough; and he recovers self-respect in hopeless defiance of his tyrants. With just a little luck though, he need never have lost it. He is blinded and turned helpless from his own doors. Is this poetic justice upon a gentleman, whose worst fault has been to play for safety, his worst blunder to think ill of a man without question and to believe a liar? Disquieting to think that it may be! [1]

Edmund is, in wickedness, half-brother to Iago. Having no such great nature as Othello's to work on, Shakespeare has no need of such transcendent villainy; and he lessens and vulgarises his man by giving him one of those excuses for foul play against the world which a knave likes to find as a point of departure. His first soliloquy is a

[1] For an earlier stroke of irony—only to be fully appreciated perhaps by the shade of Lady Gloucester—consider the exclamation wrung from the distracted old man at the climax of his wrath against Edgar:

O strong and fasten'd villain!
Would he deny his letter? *I never got him.*

And this to Edmund his bastard!

complete enough disclosure. The fine flourish of

> Thou, Nature, art my goddess . . .

(finer by its surprise for us in the mouth of the modest young man of the earlier scene), and the magnificent rejection of conventional morality narrow to their objective in

> Well then,
> Legitimate Edgar, I must have your land.

And from this firm business-like basis Edmund, except for pure pose, never soars again. The later

> This is the excellent foppery of the world . . .

is enjoyable argument, no doubt, and doubtless he chuckles over it. There is a sporting and imaginative touch, perhaps, in the trick that finally gets rid of Edgar; the stabbing his own arm, we feel, is to his credit. But for the rest, a strict attention to business, and a quick eye to one main chance after the other, suffice him. And this, really, is almost the loathliest thing about the man. He not only betrays his father to Cornwall, but he cants about loyalty the while. He accepts the attentions of Regan and Goneril without surprise or embarrassment (he is a handsome young fellow and he knows it), calculates which will be the more desirable connection, but will leave Goneril to get rid of her husband alone if that risky task has to be undertaken. It even passes through his mind that she herself—if not Regan—may in her turn have to be ' put away.' His tardy repentance does not touch us.[1] The

---

[1] His " Ask me not what I know," in which he takes example from Goneril—and Iago!—is given by one Quarto and some editors to Goneril herself, with (I fancy) good enough reason.

207

queer snobbery which prompts him to say to the still visored Edgar

> If thou'rt noble,
> I do forgive thee,

and the still queerer vanity (at such a moment!) of

> Yet Edmund was beloved.
> The one the other poison'd for my sake,
> And after slew herself,

may strike upon some ears as all but ridiculous. He is an ignoble scoundrel and he makes an ignoble end.

Still, his methods have been interesting. The first attack upon his father's credulity was, as we saw, both bold and apt; and what could be safer support to the fiction of Edgar's plot than the counterfeit truth of

> When I dissuaded him from his intent . . .
>   he replied,
> Thou unpossessing bastard! dost thou think,
> If I would stand against thee, would the reposal
> Of any trust, virtue, or worth in thee
> Make thy words faith'd? No: what I should deny,—
> As this I would; ay, though thou didst produce
> My very character, I'd turn it all
> To thy suggestion, plot, and damned practice.

For masterly confounding of counsel this should rouse the admiration of the most practised liar. Whether, later, there is need for him to be so snivellingly hypocritical with Cornwall we may question. But he is still on promotion; and that shrewd, forthright brute, if not deceived, will be the more flattered by this tribute of vice to his virtue.

But once he is in the saddle, and when not one

royal lady, but two, have lost their heads over him, what a change!

> Know of the Duke if his last purpose hold,
> Or whether since he is advised by aught
> To change his course; he's full of alteration
> And self-reproving; bring his constant pleasure.

This he says publicly of no less a man than Albany, whom later he salutes with an ironically patronising

> Sir, you speak nobly.

He is losing his head, one fears, in the flush of his fire-new fortune. Albany, however, waits his time and prepares for it; this mild gentleman should have been better reckoned with. For, of a sudden, Edmund finds that he has climbed, even as his blinded father set out in misery to climb, to the edge of a steep. And it is an apposite phrase indeed which flashes the depths on him:

> Half-blooded fellow, yes!

—from an Albany not so mild. The wheel is coming circle.

This individual catastrophe and its contriving are a good example of Shakespeare's adapting of end to means (that constant obligation of the dramatist), and of his turning disability to advantage. His very need to compress close these latter incidents of Edmund's rise to fortune helps him make it the more egregious. The fact that but a dozen speeches seem to lift the fellow towards the grasping of the very power of which Lear divested himself at the play's beginning should make our recollection of that modest young man in the background of its first scene the more amazing to us. It is, at this juncture, a breathless business for all concerned. Then at the climax comes the sudden isolation of the upstart, brave in his armour, flushed with his triumph. And Shakespeare releases the tension—and rewards himself for his economy—in the sounding of trumpets, the fine flow and colour of some heroic verse quite in his old style, and all the exciting ceremony of the duel.[1] Late in the play as this comes, and of secondary concern to the greater tragedy as it may be, not a point of its thriftily developed drama must be missed.

Edgar is a ' slow starter ' and shows no promise at all as a hero. Not here, however, but in Shakespeare's use of him as Poor Tom will be the actor's greater handicap. For by the time he is free from this arbitrary bondage the play has put our attention and emotions to some strain and we are no longer so well disposed to the development of a fresh serious interest. Otherwise there is every dramatic fitness in his tardy coming to his own. Edmund flashes upon us in pinchbeck brilliance; the worth of Edgar waits discovery, and trial and misfortune must help discover it— to himself above all.

> . . . a brother noble,
> Whose nature is so far from doing harms
> That he suspects none; on whose foolish honesty
> My practices ride easy !

says Edmund of him in proper contempt. " What are you ? " asks his unknowing father, when

[1] Compare the ' defiances ' of this scene with the passage between Mowbray and Norfolk in the beginning of *Richard II.*

his fortunes are still at their worst. And he answers:

> A most poor man, made tame to fortune's blows;
> Who, by the art of known and feeling sorrows,
> Am pregnant to good pity.

But, by the play's end, it is to him as well as to Kent that Albany turns with

> Friends of my soul, you twain,
> Rule in this realm, and the gor'd state sustain.

What are the steps by which he passes from nobody to somebody?

His very reserve at the beginning can give him a stamp of distinction, and should be made to do so. And the notion of that strange disguise would not come, we may say, to a commonplace man. Through the ravings of Poor Tom we can detect something of the mind of Edgar with its misprision of the sensual life—of his father's life, is it? We can certainly see his pitiful heart; this Shakespeare stresses. But only in the soliloquies that end Act III, Scene vi, and begin Act IV do we discover the full mind of the man: [1]

> When we our betters see bearing our woes,
> We scarcely think our miseries our foes.
> Who alone suffers, suffers most i' the mind,
> Leaving free things and happy shows behind;
> But then the mind much sufferance doth o'erskip,
> When grief hath mates, and bearing fellowship,

and

> Yet better thus, and known to be contemn'd,
> Than still contemn'd and flatter'd. To be worst,

---

[1] The Folio rejects the first of those two and (see p. 150, note) the producer may be wise to.

> The lowest and most dejected thing of fortune,
> Stands still in esperance, lives not in fear;
> The lamentable change is from the best;
> The worst returns to laughter.

We seem to have found the play's philosopher. And the sententiousness of the first soliloquy, differing both in form and tone from anything that has preceded it in the play, is surely a deliberate contrivance to lower the tension of the action and to prepare us for the calmer atmosphere—by comparison—of the play's ending. Shakespeare may afterwards have repented of it as sounding too sententious and as coming uselessly for its wider purpose immediately before the blinding of Gloucester. But Edgar's philosophy of indifference to fortune, of patience with life itself, of the good comfort of fellowship, is now, certainly, to dominate the play. It is summed up for us more than once.

> Bear free and patient thoughts,

he tells his father, when, by his queer stratagem—again, it was not the notion of a commonplace mind—he has saved him from despair. His playing the peasant with the insufferable Oswald is, yet again, not commonplace; and, having killed him:

> He is dead. I am only sorry
> He had no other deathsman.[1]

---

[1] " Chill pick your teeth, sir," suggests that he stabs him, either with a knife he wears, or, possibly, with Oswald's own dagger, wrested after a tussle.

212

To him is given the answer to Gloucester's deadly

> As flies to wanton boys, are we to the gods;
> They kill us for their sport,

in

> . . . therefore, thou happy father,
> Think that the clearest gods, who make them honours
> Of men's impossibilities, have preserved thee.

To him is given

> The gods are just, and of our pleasant vices
> Make instruments to plague us.

But before this, his good name and his father's death justly avenged, what is the first thing he says as he discloses himself to the doubly damned scoundrel lying at his feet?

> Let's exchange charity.

Edgar, in fact, has become a man of character indeed, modest, of a discerning mind, and, in this pagan play, a very Christian gentleman.[1]

Burgundy, France, Albany, Cornwall.

Burgundy and France hardly outpass convention, though the one gains enough character from his laconic indifference, while the spirit and quality

[1] He is, I think, as true a gentleman as the plays give us. And he is kept himself and no mere moraliser to the last. When Lear sinks dying, it is Edgar who starts forward to recover him, till Kent checks him with the immortal

> Vex not his ghost: O, let him pass, he hates him
> That would upon the rack of this tough world
> Stretch him out longer.

For Edgar is still very young.

of France's speeches should keep him a pleasant
memory to the play's end.[1]

Cornwall has 'character' in abundance. He
and Albany stand all but mute at their first
appearance.[2] But from our next sight of him to
our last he justifies in action and speech Gloucester's
description:

> My dear lord,
> You know the fiery quality of the duke;
> How unremoveable and fix'd he is
> To his own course.

He is a man, we may suppose, in the prime of life;
old enough, at least, to say to Edmund

> . . . thou shalt find a dearer father in my love.

He is by no means a stupid man: the cynical
humour with which he appraises Kent proves that.
He asserts himself against his wife as Albany does
not. He can speak up to Lear when need be, but
he is not too swift to do it. In his vindictiveness
he still keeps his head.

> Go seek the traitor Gloucester,
> Pinion him like a thief, bring him before us.
> Though well we may not pass upon his life

---

[1] Here is one of the difficulties incidental to the production
of such a play as *King Lear* with a company gathered in for
the occasion. The quality of the actors available tends to
diminish with the importance of the parts. Pay apart, an
actor of authority and distinction will not attach himself
to a theatre for the sole purpose of playing France. Hence
the need of an established company with all its compensating
opportunities. France is a powerful king and Cordelia's
husband; and if he does not impress us as he should, and
lodge himself in our memories, not only is the play immediately the poorer, but Cordelia, returning, is robbed of a
background of great importance to her.

[2] By the text of the Quarto absolutely mute.

> Without the form of justice, yet our power
> Shall do a courtesy to our wrath, which men
> May blame but not control.

But this hardly makes him the more likeable. And though we might allow him some credit for at least doing his own dirty work, it is evident that he enjoys Gloucester's blinding, for he sets about it with a savage jest. The taste of blood seems to let loose all the wild beast in him; and, like a wild beast, Shakespeare has him despatched. Yet Cornwall is a forceful character; and there are those who—having no more concern with them than to profit by their forcefulness—can find, strangely enough, something to admire in such men. So he may be allowed a certain dog-toothed attractiveness in performance.

Albany is at the opposite pole. He prefers a quiet life with Goneril while he can contrive to lead it, even at the cost of some self-respect.

> Striving to better, oft we mar what's well,

seems to stand as his motto; and it sounds the more sententious by its setting in a rhymed couplet. His " milky gentleness," his " harmful mildness " ring true enough as accusations: does he think to tame a tigress with a platitude? His wife, quite naturally, departs to seek Regan's help without him.

Much has happened, though, by the time we see him again, when Goneril is on the full tide of reckless triumphant wickedness. She takes no heed of Oswald's

> . . . never man so changed,

still presumes on

> . . . the cowish terror of his spirit,

and even, when she meets him changed indeed, is blind and deaf to the change. That Albany had loved his wife is made plain. We hear him speak in his quiet way of " the great love " he bore her. He has been slow to think ill of her. But he is of those who let their wrath gather beneath a placid surface till, on a sudden, it boils over, and if the cause of their wrath has lain deep they are never the same again. Shakespeare, who cannot spare much space for his development, gives us this impression of the man by giving us these contrasted sights of him, the long interval between. And the first stern clash with Goneril has a double purpose and nets a double dramatic gain. It wins Albany the authoritative standing that he now needs to have in the play, and it shows us a Goneril so possessed by self-will that our own surprise at the change in him turns to surprise that she can be so oblivious of it. We may count her a doomed creature from this moment.

Henceforth he is pitted against Edmund; the aristocrat against the upstart; the man with nothing to gain against the man who must win and still win or perish; the man who, to the taunt of " moral fool," can answer

> Where I could not be honest,
> I never yet was valiant:

against the man who can tell his follower as he sends him to commit an atrocious murder:

> . . . know thou this, that men
> Are as the time is; to be tender-minded
> Does not become a sword; thy great employment
> Will not bear question; either say thou'lt do 't,
> Or thrive by other means.

The world's allegiance is ever swaying between such leaderships.

Albany, once in action, is as distinguished a figure as any in the play. Shakespeare dowers him with a fine sense of irony. The slight sting in the tail of his compliment to Edmund after the battle:

> Sir, you have showed to-day your valiant strain,
> And fortune led you well;

the cutting courtesy of

> Sir, by your patience,
> I hold you but a subject of this war,
> Not as a brother,

his cool preparation of his stroke; the stroke itself:

> Stay yet, hear reason. Edmund, I arrest thee
> On capital treason; and, in thy arrest,
> This gilded serpent. For your claim, fair sister,
> I bar it in the interest of my wife;
> 'Tis she is sub-contracted to this lord,
> And I, her husband, contradict your banns.
> If you will marry, make your loves to me,
> My lady is bespoke

—are not bad for a moral fool.

Nor does he trust to the appearance of the unknown champion for Edmund's undoing. He throws his own gauntlet down. A touch of gallantry, though Shakespeare does not—does not need to—compromise his dignity by setting him to fight. And he is left from now to the play's end in command of its action.[1]

---

[1] Though the last speech should probably, in accordance with the Folio, be Edgar's.

217

Oswald and the minor parts.

A modern audience must lose almost as much of
the flavour of Oswald as of the Fool; and more
still must be lost if he is stripped of his doublet and
hose, forbidden his swagger and his curtseys and
thrust back into the dark ages. We cannot be
expected to cheer—as I doubt not Shakespeare's
audience did—when Kent breaks out with

> That such a slave as this should wear a sword,
> Who wears no honesty!

nor to take the precise point of Lear's

> How now   where's that mongrel?

that new-fangled fellow, neither gentleman nor
plain servant, mimicking the manners of the one,
doing dirtier work than the other. Kent sizes
him up when he dresses him down, with enjoyable
completeness; so does Lear, later, in a dozen
words:

> This is a slave, whose easy-borrowed pride
> Dwells in the fickle grace of her he follows.

So does Edgar, having rid the world of him, as

> . . . a serviceable villain;
> As duteous to the vices of thy mistress
> As badness would desire.

Oswalds have existed in every age and been good
game for abuse, but the London of Shakespeare's
day had evidently produced an unusually fine crop
of them. His own sayings are colourless compared
with what is said of him. It follows, then, that
his ' Ay madams ' and ' No madams,' his " I'll not
be strucken, my lord," his " prithee, if thou lovest

me, tell me," and his " Out, dunghill," when the peasant's cudgel threatens to knock his dishonourable sword out of his hand, must answer exactly in accent and attitude, as he himself in look and manner, to the very sort of being Shakespeare had in mind. In himself he is nothing; " a whoreson zed, an unnecessary letter," and he should seem no more. But as a tailor made him he must be tailored right.

It remains to notice one or two of Shakespeare's minuter touches. When Gloucester has been blinded, branded a traitor and turned from his own house to smell his way to Dover, he finds one fearless friend; the old peasant who has been his tenant and his father's tenant " these fourscore years." The savagery of the blinding itself had stirred one common fellow to risk and lose his life stopping the worst of it. Two other common fellows have the charity to bind up the wounds; but they'll risk no more than that. The old peasant, too old himself to go far with his lord, shakes a sad head at leaving him in such company as Poor Tom, and will risk his fortunes to do Gloucester, in his ruin and disgrace, a last simple service. Close following the transcendent scenes of Lear's madness and the extreme brutality of the blinding comes this interlude of servant and peasant, of common humanity in its bravery and charity with its simple stumbling talk. The whole effect is made in a dozen lines or so, but gains importance by its homespun contrast and by its placing across the main dividing line of the play's action.

And for a happy instance of Shakespeare's power to suggest a man in a dozen words, take the reply

of the Captain to whom Edmund confides the
murder of Lear and Cordelia:

> I cannot draw a cart nor eat dried oats;
> If it be man's work, I'll do it.

STAGING AND COSTUME

No more need be urged, I hope, against a
realistic staging of the play or anything approaching one. But whether the single alternative to
this is the actuality of Shakespeare's own theatre
is another question, which the producer must
answer for himself. If he protests that his audience
will never sit so unconsciously before a reproduction of the Globe stage as did Shakespeare's
before the thing itself one cannot contradict him.
But he cuts from the anchorage at his peril. And
the doubt is as to whether when he has found some,
presumably, atmospheric sort of background, which
does not positively conflict with the play's stagecraft, the result—for all its visual beauty—will be
worth the risk and the trouble. Not actualities,
however, but principles are involved, and if the
spirit of the law can be better fulfilled by the
rewriting of its letter, why, let it be!

Abide by Shakespeare's own stage, and no
questions of importance arise upon the use of it.
But for Edgar's moment ' above,' some need for
the masking of Lear's ' state,' and again for the
discovery of the joint-stools and bench in the
scene of the mock trial, the play could indeed be
acted upon a barer stage than was the Globe's.[1]

---

[1] There are one or two signs that the stage to which the
Folio version was fitted differed a little from that of the
Quarto.

The great chair with the unconscious Lear in it may be more conveniently carried from an inner stage, and Poor Tom will emerge more effectively from one than from a sidedoor. But this is all; and it may even be that Shakespeare minimised such localisation as his theatre did afford him to give the play spaciousness of action, and to magnify his characters the more in isolating them from needless detail of circumstance. Let the producer, at any rate,—and at all costs—provide for the action's swift unencumbered movement and for our concentration upon the characters themselves, in whom everything is concentrated.

As for costume, this is one of the few plays in which Shakespeare took some trouble to do more than its subject itself would do to dissociate it from his own time; though even so he will not have relied overmuch upon costume to help him. But only here and there is his own seventeenth century patent, and that in character or incident of minor importance. The prevailing atmosphere and accent is barbaric and remote. Edmund's relationship to Iago may seem to us to give him a certain Italianate flavour, and Edgar's beginning suggests bookishness and the Renaissance. But clothe these two as we please, their substance will defy disguise. Oswald, as we have argued, is a topical picture; in the Ancient Briton he will be all but obliterated. That must be faced. Of the Fool, by shifting him back a dozen centuries, we lose little, because, as we have argued, we are bound already to lose so much. And if a Fool in a barbarous king's retinue seems to us an anachronism (though it may be doubted if—for all the preciseness that would take offence at a Henry V in doublet and hose—it will) the fantasy of the part marks it out as the fittest note of relief from consistency. To consistency in such matters no dated play of Shakespeare can be submitted. Here our main losses by desertion of seventeenth-century habit and manners will end. And such anachronism as may lie in Cordelia's chance of being Duchess of Burgundy, in " base foot-ball player " and " unfee'd lawyer," in the stocks, in some of Poor Tom's talk and Lear's ravings, and in the procedure of the challenge and the duel, will be inconsiderable however the characters are clothed.

So a producer is free to balance these items against an imagined Britain, whose king swears

   . . . by the mysteries of Hecate and the night

(not to mention Apollo), and where a duke of Cornwall turns public executioner. There is no doubt, I think, in which scale advantage lies. The play should be costumed according to the temper that Shakespeare has given it, a splendid barbaric temper. It is equally clear that archæological accuracy profits nothing. Nor should the producer lose more than he need of such sophistication as Shakespeare himself retained.

THE MUSIC

About the music there is little to be said. I do not imagine much improvement possible upon " the consort of viols," to the quiet harmonies of which Lear was meant, one presumes, to be waked. The sennet that announces his first regal appearance should be noted, as well as the flourish to herald France and Burgundy, and the ceremonial difference between the two. The 'horns within,' which prelude Lear's return from hunting ask no comment. A trumpet is used with dramatic effect before Cornwall's entrance in Act II, Scene i; it reinforces Gloucester's excitement. The same sound stirs Lear a little later and strings him up for the encounter with Goneril. And, towards the play's end, the triple sounding by the herald, to be answered, when our suspense is keenest, by Edgar's trumpet without, is a most carefully calculated dramatic effect.[1] We have noticed earlier how the battle in which Cordelia's forces are defeated is dramatically minimised; its musical symbolism consists only of an alarum and an alarum and retreat. But the " drum afar off," to the ominous sound of which the longest and most varied scene of the fourth act closes, has very definite value. So has the dead march with which the play itself ends.

The Fool is allotted no formal and completed song, but, needless to say, his snatches of melody should be melodious indeed. This musical and lyrical relief to the strain of Lear's passion is, as we have argued elsewhere, an essential part of the play's stagecraft. The technique of the singing should not be artificial; rather that of an accomplished folk-song singer. And where no authentically traditional tunes exist, folk music will prove a sufficient quarry.

THE TEXT

The complications of the text are troublesome. Corruptions, obvious and suspected, apart, the

---

[1] Beethoven found a similar one useful in *Fidelio*.

producer is confronted by the problem of the
three hundred lines, or nearly, that the Quartos
give and the Folio omits, and of the hundred
given by the Folio and omitted from the Quartos.
Editors, considering only, it would seem, that the
more Shakespeare we get the better, bring practically the whole lot into the play we read. But a
producer must ask himself whether these two
versions do not come from different prompt
books, and whether the Folio does not, both in cuts
and additions, sometimes represent Shakespeare's
own second thoughts. In general, surely, the
Folio is of better authority; it is at least more
carefully transcribed. Some of its cuts are of
passages which seem to have been found con-
structionally unnecessary. Some only ' ease ' the
dialogue; they are of varying importance and
aptness. Where Quarto and Folio offer alter-
natives, to adopt both versions may make for
redundancy or confusion.[1]

To deal with the major differences. In the
scene of the dividing of the kingdom the Folio's
stressed identification of Albany and Cornwall,
France and Burgundy, seems deliberate and is
certainly valuable. Of the additions to the
Gloucester–Edmund–Edgar scene the same may
be said. Gloucester can hardly be shown too
distracted, and the hiding away of Edgar from his
father is a good point made But, in compensation,
the Folio cuts the mockery of Gloucester's foibles
with which Edmund preludes his attempt on
Edgar's confidence—and one sees why.

[1] I speak from now on of ' the Quarto ' because for the
purposes of this argument the ' Pied Bull ' and ' Butter '
Quartos might be one.

In Goneril's first scene with Oswald the Folio's omissions save some repetition and show her to us terser and less familiar with her servant. A Folio cut in the Fool's part a little later—his rhyming upon the " sweet and bitter fool," and the joke about monopolising—maybe seem at a first glance a little clumsy. But we shall hardly appreciate the gibe at monopolies unless we re-write it ' trusts '; probably the Quarto's audiences had appreciated it too well The whole cut is a useful tightening of the dialogue. Yet a little later the Folio gives us (as the Quarto does not) a passage in which Goneril justifies herself to Albany; undoubtedly useful.

When Lear finds Kent in the stocks and has listened in silence to the story of his being set there, by the Quarto

> O, how this mother swells up toward my heart

follows immediately upon Kent's story. The Folio gives the Fool a little piping song, while Lear still stands speechless, his agony upon him. The dramatic effect will be appreciably different.

Later the Folio alone gives us a passage in which Regan justifies Goneril.

In Act III, Scene i, the Folio cuts some important lines out of the Gentleman's second speech. In particular

> . . . Strives in his little world of man to outscorn
> The to-and-fro-conflicting wind and rain,

has vanished. An inefficient actor might have been the cause of this. A few lines later Folio and Quarto offer us alternative cuts. That of the Folio is perhaps the clumsier of the two. It stresses the call for Cordelia's help but barely hints

225

at her army's landing, which the Quarto emphasises. We may or may not have here the cutting of a common original (of which still more may have existed; for of the

> . . . servants, who seem no less,
> Which are to France the spies and speculations
> Intelligent of our state

we do not hear again). The object of the cut in both cases—and possibly the cutting of the Gentleman's speech also—is evidently to shorten this prelude to Lear's great entrance. What should a producer do here? Shakespeare leaves us to the end a little unconvinced by the machinery of Cordelia's return. There is no dramatic profit in the confusion. Neither text may be as Shakespeare left it. But in this instance I prefer the Quarto's to an amalgam of the two.

Of Merlin's prophecy I have spoken elsewhere.

Let us in passing note the Folio's most important addition of two lines preparation for the critical

> Poor naked wretches, wheresoe'er you are . . .

In them the kindness to the half-drowned Fool is emphasised; and he is (I think) sent off the stage so that there may be no danger whatever of discord or incongruity. The actor of the Fool, possibly, was never quite to be relied on; and even if he could be, there was always the chance that some buffoon in the audience would vent an incongruous guffaw at the mere sight of him sitting there. But, above all, by these two lines the meaning and intention of what is to come are emphasised:

> In, boy, go first. You houseless poverty—
> Nay, get thee in. *I'll pray and then I'll sleep.*

226

I italicise the vitally important phrase. It is
dangerous to dogmatise; but this addition has
to me all the air of being a second thought of
Shakespeare's own.

We come to the Folio's omission of the mock
trial. One can only suppose that in acting it had
proved ineffective. One cannot imagine Shakespeare regretting he had written it.

The cut at the end of this scene, however, asks
more consideration; for a purely dramatic reason
can be found for the omission of Edgar's soliloquy.
It must lower the tension of the action. This
may damage the scene of Gloucester's blinding,
which follows immediately; and if an act pause
is to follow, the tension will, of course, be lowered
then. The chief purpose of the soliloquy, moreover, is to give Edgar a fresh start in his dramatic
life. It is a quiet start, the effect of which the
violent scene that follows must do much to
obliterate. When the Folio, then, postpones it to
the beginning of Act IV, it does Edgar a double
service, as the Quarto doubles the disservice by
making the second soliloquy, when it comes,
seem dramatically redundant. Without hesita-
tion, I should here follow the Folio text. The
further cutting of Kent's lines, however,

Oppressed nature sleeps . . .

is probably due to a quick closing of the inner
stage, which may have obviated the lifting of the
sleeping Lear, and it has not the same validity.

The Folio also cuts the significant piece of
dialogue between the two servants with which
the third act ends. I cannot pretend to say why,
if it was not that when this text was settled, the

16

actors to speak the lines were lacking. No one need abide by this cut.

The disappearance of Edgar's "Obidicut, Hobbididance" and the rest from the first scene with his father is, I think, to the good. A few lines before he says:

I cannot daub it further.

And in any case the effect of the mad lingo will have been exhausted in the scenes with Lear.

We next come to some ruthless cutting of Albany by the Folio. Shakespeare may have yielded here to the exigencies of bad acting or to a wish to knit the action more closely. But he is taking some pains at this juncture to develop Albany, and we shall be on the safe side in keeping to the fuller text.

Now, however, the Folio omits one entire scene. It is a carpentered scene if ever there was one. It begins with a lame explanation of the non-appearance of the King of France; it goes on to a preparation for the reappearance of Cordelia and it ends with some unconvincing talk about Lear's shame and Kent's disguise. I could better believe that Shakespeare cut it than wrote it. There is, certainly, a little life in the description of Cordelia, and a case can be made for so heralding her return to the play. The rest is explanation of what is better left unexplained; and whoever, between the making of the Quarto and the Folio, discovered this—Shakespeare or another—did the play a good service, which we shall wisely profit by.

The remaining differences between the two versions show, in the Folio, a further cutting of explanatory stuff, by which we may well abide; a certain slicing into Albany and Edmund that neither hurts them much now, nor, it is true, does much to spur the action; the loss of one or two lines (Cordelia's in particular) that we shall not want to lose, and the gain of a few that seem good second thoughts. There are, besides, one or two changes that seem merely to reflect change in stage practice as between Quarto and Folio.

On the whole, then—and if he show a courageous discretion—I recommend a producer to found himself on the Folio. For that it does show some at least of Shakespeare's own re-shapings I feel sure.

Among other slightly vexed questions, the following are particularly worth attention (the lineal references are to the Arden Shakespeare).

Act I, Scene i, 35. There is no authority for Edmund's exit, and the producer is quite at liberty to let him stay and listen to the momentous proceedings.

Scene v, 1. I give a guess that ' Gloucester ' in this line is a slip for ' Cornwall.' There is no other evidence that Lear writes to the Earl of Gloucester, nor any reason he should, nor any evidence at all that Cornwall lived near the town.

52-3. This couplet has the sanction (as Merlin's prophecy has not) of both Quarto and Folio. But I find its authenticity hard to credit. Shakespeare could write bawdry, and sometimes at what seem to us the unlikeliest moments. This does not smack of the Fool, though, or of what Shakespeare wants of him.

Act II, Scene i, 20. *Enter Edgar.* This stage direction is wrongly placed—and typically—in modern editions. The Quarto places it four lines, the Folio a line, earlier. Even the Folio, then, shows that he enters on the upper stage and is visible to the audience before Edmund sees him. It may seem a small matter,

KING LEAR

but the difference between an independent entrance and being called on like a dog is appreciable, and can affect a character's importance. Edgar does descend, of course.

Scene ii, 168–73. "Nothing almost sees miracles, But misery . . . and shall find time From this enormous state, seeking to give Losses their remedies." Cut this much, and an actor can make sense of a passage otherwise as obscure as it is evidently corrupt.

Scene iii. I think, on the whole, that there is no scene-division here; there is not, that is to say, a cleared stage. Curtains might be drawn before Kent in the stocks, but he may as well sit there asleep while Edgar soliloquises. On an *unlocalised* stage I doubt its puzzling even a modern audience if he does; it certainly would not have troubled Shakespeare's.

Act III, Scene iii. The Quarto stage-direction *Enter . . . with lights* shows, I think, if nothing else does, the use of the inner stage for this scene.

Scene vii, 23. Neither Quarto nor Folio specifies Oswald's exit, and they get Edmund's and Goneril's wrong. But it is plain that Oswald should be gone immediately on the command to get horses for his mistress. Edmund's and Goneril's leave-taking then stands out the plainer, and the "strange œilliads and most speaking looks" that pass between them as they go may be made noticeable to Regan—and to us.

Act IV, Scene iv, 6. 'Centurie' says the Quarto and 'centery' the Folio; and this surely will be understood even now (and whatever the anachronism) to mean a hundred men. Why send one sentry to look for Lear? And why a sentry, anyhow?

Act V, Scene iii, 161. "Ask me not what I know." The Quarto gives this to Goneril and marks her exit accordingly. It is at least a question whether the Folio's change is not erroneous. For Edmund's so sudden change of front is not easily explicable.

284. This is the first and only indication that Kent's name in disguise has been Caius. And I cannot discover that any editor has commented upon the strangeness of Kent—Kent of all people, and at

230

this moment of all others—asking Lear a kind of conundrum. The Pied Bull Quarto at least gives no note of interrogation. And if the line can be spoken as if it meant

Your servant Kent, who was your servant Caius,

it will at least not jar. Leave it a question and Lear's answer seems to apply to Caius, whereas Kent's next line makes it clearly a reference to Kent.

324. The Quarto gives the last speech to Albany, the Folio to Edgar. Convention would allot it to Albany as the man of rank. " We that are young " sounds more like Edgar. But remembering how much Albany's part is cut in the Folio, it is likely, I think, that this change was deliberately made—if indeed the Quarto attribution is not erroneous anyhow—and therefore it should stand.